The Incubation Workbook

The Incubation Workbook

navigating innovation from concept to commercialization

Arizona Center for Innovation
Office of University Research Parks

The Incubation Workbook: Navigating Innovation from Concept to Commercialization

Published by Wheatmark®
1760 East River Road, Suite 145
Tucson, Arizona 85718
www.wheatmark.com

ISBN: 978-1-60494-703-8
LCCN: 2011937524

The Arizona Center for Innovation was founded with the help of many who have contributed their ideas, time, energy, and assistance. This book is dedicated to them:

Jim Fountain
Molly Gilbert
Bob Hagen
Henry Koffler
Bo Statham
Marie Wesselhoft
Bruce Wright

Contents

Congratulations!

If you are reviewing this workbook, you have taken the next step to building your new venture.

This workbook was designed as a resource to help technology incubator clients navigate the innovation continuum from concept to market commercialization. It can be used as an independent reference, as a checklist and foundation for an entrepreneur's journal, or as a companion for workshops and mentor sessions.

If you are engaged with the Arizona Center for Innovation, you will find additional and supplemental content at: www.azinnovation.com. If you are not currently engaged with an incubator, this workbook will provide you with an introduction to the incubator experience, and our team would be more than happy to recommend an incubator in your area.

We invite you to use this book as your entrepreneur's journal; you can use it as a resource to brainstorm new ideas, take notes, organize thoughts, and track your progress. It provides general information and checklists on a variety of key topics targeted toward technology start-up ventures, and it includes additional tips and tools designed to help you create a long-term plan for success. If you are an incubator client, bring this workbook with you when you next meet with your mentors and advisors.

Thank you for allowing us to share our experiences with you. We wish you the best success with your new venture.

Best regards,

Bruce Wright
President, Arizona Center for Innovation

Starting with Success

Getting the most from your experience with an incubator

About Business Incubation

According to the National Business Incubation Association (www.nbia.org), business incubation got its start in the early 1950s with the concept of "providing business assistance services to early-stage companies in shared facilities."[1] By the early 1980s, approximately twelve incubators had been established in the United States. Through promotion by the U.S. Small Business Administration, successes from the first technology incubators, community support, and investor participation, the number of incubators swelled to over 1,400 in North America by 2006, and 7,000 worldwide. About 39 percent of all incubators focus just on technology.

Why Use an Incubator?

Other interesting NBIA facts include the following:[2]
  » "In 2005 alone, North American incubators assisted more than 27,000 start-up companies that provided full-time employment for more than 100,000 workers and generated annual revenue of more than $17 billion."
  » "Business incubators reduce the risk of small business failures. Historically, NBIA member incubators have reported that 87 percent of all firms that have graduated from their incubators are still in business."
  » "Research has shown that for every $1 of estimated public operating subsidy provided the incubator, clients and graduates of NBIA member incubators generate approximately $30 in local tax revenue alone."
  » "NBIA members have reported that 84 percent of incubator graduates stay in their communities."

---

1   National Business Incubation Association, "The History of Business Incubation" http://www.nbia.org/resource_library/history/index.php 2006 State of the Business Incubation Industry Report
2   http://www.nbia.org/resource_library/faq/index.php#3

Typically, companies that successfully move through the incubation process and graduate are more likely to develop successful and sustainable ventures that remain in the community. These companies bring new technologies and products to market; they create jobs and wealth in the community; and they have the ability to positively influence our world.

Incubators: What to Look For

If you are not yet part of an incubator and considering joining one, look for an incubator that:
» provides the complementary services and support you need for your venture;
» has membership in a national organization such as the National Business Incubation Association (www.nbia.org) to ensure best practices and to provide a larger network of resources;
» has a proven track record with successful graduates;
» has a strong network of partnerships in your community; and
» has an experienced team.

Incubators should provide you with a wide range of support services. The following list is taken from the Arizona Center for Innovation (AzCI), so use this as a general guideline and check with the incubator in your area for specific details.

Services provided by the Arizona Center for Innovation (AzCI) include:
» triage of the venture and technology to create a customized program of training and support;
» workshops and virtual training on a variety of business topics led by content experts;
» calendar of related community events;
» group coaching;
» one-on-one mentoring;
» leadership training;
» executive strategy sessions and brainstorming events;
» Advisory Committee formation;
» practice presentation and pitch sessions;
» assistance with fund-raising plans;
» assistance with product prototype planning;
» access to professional service providers that may provide pro bono or discounted services;
» a true plug-and-play environment including a part-time receptionist, mail service, copy center, desk with phone, high-speed internet, meeting rooms, office space, kitchen, and in some cases catering services;
» access to wet and dry lab space, specialty equipment, chemical storage, and a lab manager;
» elbow space with other entrepreneurs experiencing similar situations;
» prestige and instant credibility of being accepted in to a successful incubator; and
» general support and cheerleading.

As a general rule, most incubators provide exceptional support, but it's up to you, the entrepreneur, to take advantage of whatever programs and services are provided.

Admissions to an Incubator

Joining an incubator is a big commitment for everyone involved. The magic of incubation starts with the right number of ventures, an interesting and complementary mix of projects, and a strong ratio of appropriate partners (advisors and mentors) to entrepreneurs. Therefore, most incubators have a formal admissions process and will take a little extra time to determine whether your specific needs can be met. This also ensures a right fit for everyone.

Acceptance to an incubator is a significant milestone in your venture development. The right incubator partnership can give you instant credibility and key partnerships, and it can lead to your success happening more quickly.

Ideal Incubator Clients

How do you know if you are a right candidate for an incubator? In general, ideal incubator clients:
- » need, and have the ability to benefit from, incubator services;
- » have a management team capable of handling technical and operational aspects of the business and the willingness to obtain assistance where appropriate;
- » are in start-up operational mode with the ability to pay incubator fees where appropriate;
- » can demonstrate the ability to provide economic benefits in the form of job and wealth creation or otherwise develop a product or service that will benefit the region (in many cases a local operational presence is also required);
- » should not be in direct competition with an existing incubator client;
- » demonstrate technology-driven innovation that may lend itself to a scalable and sustainable business (for a technology-specific incubator);
- » complete the application process; and
- » must successfully complete an admissions interview with the review team.

What to Expect

Once admitted to an incubator, you should ask to establish an immediate course of action for workshops, training, mentoring, and a list of actions and milestones. This helps your incubator team understand what resources you need and keeps you both on track and moving forward.

It's also important to note that many incubators are required to report total statistics, including number of companies, employees, dollars raised, revenues, etc. In most cases this is a general report and does not disclose information by company. However, it does mean that you may be asked for regular reporting details.

Your incubator-client agreement most likely includes a confidentiality agreement, so your information will be protected.

The incubation experience is different for everyone. The focus is on venture creation and success, but in many cases it is also about helping you make the transition from inventor to entrepreneur, from entrepreneur to successful business executive, or from successful entrepreneur to serial success! In general, incubators are designed to help you progress through their program as quickly and efficiently as needed for your business. The average time might take two years, but for some it may be a few months and for others several years. It all depends on your venture needs and on the commitment your team invests.

How to Make the Most of Your Incubator Experience

This is a true experiential process, and you are encouraged to take advantage of as many programs and offerings as possible. But first, consider this story based on Japanese lore:[3]

In a remote village in Japan lived the wise Master. People from all over the world would seek him out for advice and wisdom, and he seldom turned anyone away. One day, an accomplished man approached the Master to learn all that he could about the world. The Master invited him in, and the man sat as the Master began to pour his tea. The man spoke of his training, and the tea neared the brim of his cup. The man spoke of his accomplishments while the Master continued to pour the tea. Suddenly the man looked down as the tea spilled over his cup and on to the floor, and cried out: "Enough! My cup is overflowing!" The Master looked at the man, nodded in agreement, and replied, "Yes, your cup is full. Come back when it is empty."

Please don't take this as a suggestion that your cup should be empty when you join an incubator; after all, you are the content expert in your business! But leave a little room to learn something new. Every start-up company experience is unique. You will find similarities with other companies in the road map to success, but the path varies. There are differences in the technology, risks, distribution, partnerships, team abilities, market, etc. The most successful entrepreneurs look at every situation differently to discover new innovations and opportunities. To do so, you need to let go of your assumptions, open your mind, and be willing to learn new things. Likewise, you should be prepared to learn from your colleagues. One of the biggest values of being in an incubator is simply not being alone. It's about sharing ideas, referrals, best practices, experiences, and sometimes just a cup of coffee (or tea) with others who are going through a similar experience at the same time.

This is an important note, so read it twice: *life does not stop when you start a business.*

It may be a quiet start without any fanfare. Your family, job, and whatever else surrounds you in life continues to move forward, and your new company may add or change the mix.

One other thing to keep in mind as you set expectations about working with an incubator is that your business is still *your* business. You are always in the driver's seat. The role of your incubator is to provide advice, guidance, and support. You will still do the heavy lifting - but you'll have help along the way.

Top 10 Ways to Find Success - Advice from an Incubator

Here's a fun list of ideas to help you find success in your business and get the most out of your partnership with your incubator:

1. Take ownership.

Your first action after you've been accepted should be to attend orientation - get familiar with the landscape and with any keys or badges or other important details. And then, move in! Commit at least a few

---

3   There are many sources for this story. This version is a summary of the story told by an instructor at Cortiva Institute during student orientation.

hours per week to being at the incubator if the opportunity is available; this should be dedicated time to your business. This is also a great way to build mindshare with mentors, other incubator companies and the incubator staff and partners. The more the incubator team sees you take ownership in your venture, the more excited they will become to help. Always remember, this is *your* company, and *you* are in the driver's seat.

2. Create a road map.

It's fun to visualize and think about where you want your company to be in three to five years or longer, and of course that's an important element of your success. Maybe you have a destination in mind, but how will you get there without a map? It can be overwhelming for some, so to make this easy, break it up into small bites of time. Write down what you want to accomplish in thirty days, three months, and six months. Use the AzCI benchmark table in this book to identify what steps you think you need to take next. Be proactive, and meet with a mentor or join a group coaching session as quickly as possible. This will help you assess your plan and make recommendations for training, workshops, events, etc. Take your road map and turn it into simple to-do lists.

3. Keep your eyes on the road.

This is where the road gets treacherous; on one side you'll see the scenery stretch out before you for miles with endless blue skies. You'll want to get lost in the daydream of your business, to spend hours brain-storming and strategizing and imagining what it will be like to be wildly successful. On the other side of the road, however, you'll see nothing but tall dark weeds that block out the light and demand all of your attention. These are the little and often demanding details that can absorb your time and cause you to get lost or lose sight of your goals. You don't want to step too closely to either side and forget you're on the road! Break old habits and post your to-do list in a new way: large print, in color, sticky notes on the wall, or whatever you think might work for you. Keep the list simple. Think about the top three things you need to do this month, this week, or this minute. If you feel you're stuck on either side of the road, ask for help - most incubator mentors come with a towing package.

4. Celebrate accomplishments.

Starting a business is tough, and finding balance in your life may be even tougher. If it were easy, everyone would do it! Someone once said, "Many of us can't see the forest for the trees. Entrepreneurs, however, sometimes can't even see the bark." You live, eat, sleep, drink, breathe, dream, love, and *become* your business. That passion will serve you well, but it could also lead you to early burnout. You need to take time to pop your head up and recognize that things are moving forward and that you've made accomplishments. This gives you a little pep; it engages your family and friends in your adventure, and it helps you describe the *value* you are building for your potential partners and investors.

5. Build a strong support system.

You are only one person, and in order for your company to be successful, it needs to become bigger than you. This may be hard to hear; after all, this is your idea, your passion, and no one is suggesting you give that up. However, if you want to build a successful company, it needs to become more than just you! Invest in building a team of advisors, mentors, experts, cheerleaders, supporters, and fellow adventurers. There are many ways to do this without money, as you'll learn in your incubator sessions. The one thing you can already do now is to *communicate well.* Start a blog or a newsletter. Put together a target list of folks you want to attract to your company, and send them updates on your progress. Regular communication and demonstrated progress, combined with your natural passion and enthusiasm, creates a compelling invitation to support your company. This could lead to volunteers, advisors, partners, investors, and so on. Get them on your bandwagon early.

6. Do your homework.

Your business communication is like an iceberg. At the very tip, you may touch on a few key points of your business in twenty-five or fifty words. Immediately below this is your elevator pitch, a one minute summary of your business. Below that might be an executive summary or simple one-page collateral document describing your product. Further below might be your presentations. And just above the water line is your business plan. Each piece is somewhat larger than the piece above. But if you've ever seen an iceberg, or pictures of one, you'll know that the true substance falls below the water line. This is your business plan appendix, your research, your prototype testing, and your knowledge and expertise. Even the infamous business plan napkin presentations of the Silicon Valley days were still the result of endless hours of research, discussion, and consideration before they hit the coffee shops. While you can improve your chances of success by working in an incubator, you still need to roll up your sleeves. There are no shortcuts!

7. Less is more, but you need more to have less!

You will always need to know more about your business - you are the expert, after all - but you need to say less about that more. Got it? Invest time in articulating your idea; distill key points and practice your pitch and presentation from the first day you enter the incubator. The value of your pitch is not necessarily *your* ability to deliver it, but rather the ability of *others* to deliver it. They need to easily grasp the idea to see opportunities and areas where they can help; but more importantly so they can accurately tell your story. People are going to want to talk about your business, and you want to make sure they get it right. You don't want to include anything confidential in the pitch, just general facts to express the idea, strike interest, and possibly attract new partners or investors.

8. Ask for help.

Ask your incubator for help. If they can't figure it out, they'll likely be able to find someone who can. Being part of an incubator opens doors to which you may not have had prior access. Seize the opportunity. Compare notes with your colleagues and other incubator clients. Have they tried something in particular (like a brainstorming session or forming an Advisory Committee) that you haven't tried yet? Your incubator may be able to help you coordinate, facilitate, brainstorm, challenge, present, open doors, and of course pull you back on the road. Give them a chance to show you that they can be great cheerleaders for your company!

9. Keep good notes.

Create an entrepreneur's binder right away to save important documents, but also to collect articles, research, notes, quotes, ideas, and etc. It may be a copy of this workbook with pages tucked in, a three-ring binder, or your laptop. Whatever serves you best, but make sure you track dates and content. In the early days it may be helpful to organize things by section of your business plan (research, mission statement, etc). It may require a little investment of time as you go through the process, but it will save time as you start to put your business plan and thoughts together. It will also give you brownie points with future partners and investors, because it shows you are planning for success, and you have hard data to back up your thoughts and ideas. This is particularly important as you test your product and conduct research. Start now.

10. Execute.

If you look for them, you'll find lots of reasons *not* to start your business: it's too expensive, the technology is too difficult, you don't have enough support, there is too much competition, and so on. Be realistic about your vision and make sure you're not violating the laws of physics, but don't get dragged down by a can't-do-it attitude. Keep in mind that you are innovating - that means you're probably doing something no one else has done exactly in the same way before. So the best piece of advice we can give you is to give it a try. Get in front of your potential customers for their immediate participation and feedback; test your product and monitor your progress. If you slip, try a different approach. Many successful companies today started with a different idea or technology, or made big changes along the way. Give yourself permission to be flexible in this regard, and remember that those successful companies have at least one thing in common with you: they all started somewhere.

Company or Crusade?

Here is another piece of tough love for your consideration. Are you building a company, or fighting a crusade? There is nothing wrong with fighting a crusade, but a company may be a better suited for incubation. If your focus is on building a company, create a mission statement and use that as a point of reference to help you when faced with difficult decisions. Again, remember, the company may need to become bigger than you to be successful. Build your team with people who are smarter, better, faster, more experienced than you. If your expertise is tied to the product or service, create an advisor team and consider looking for a strong CEO who can help you carry your company to the next level of success.

About the Arizona Center for Innovation

The Arizona Center for Innovation (AzCI) is a nonprofit technology business incubator in Tucson, Arizona, supporting a wide range of technologies from drug discovery to software design. One of our primary objectives is to commercialize new technology from the University of Arizona, although approximately half of the companies we serve are from the local community - demonstrating that Tucson is rich in innovation, diversity, and new venture growth. The mix between university and community research and venture development in the same incubator provides a rich experience that is unique and beneficial for everyone involved.

Our goal is to help you transform your idea into a successful new venture. This is done through a customized program of mentoring and training, access to advisors and expertise, and executive office space plus specialty equipment and laboratories. We rely heavily on a network of seasoned mentors, business and community leaders, and executives in the local community - all focused on your success. As a member of the National Business Incubation Association, AzCI can also provide additional state and national resources and best practices, increasing your resource network substantially.

AzCI provides a fun work environment, but ultimately your success is up to you. We encourage you to take advantage of the programs and services provided. We encourage you to get out of your classroom, out of your garage or pajamas, and into a real office focused on your venture development and growth. Our goal, as with any incubator, is to see your new venture move through the incubation process as quickly as possible to graduate and become a successful company that grows and contributes high-paying jobs and prosperity to the local community.

How to contact us:

Arizona Center for Innovation
9040 S. Rita Road, Suite 1270
Tucson, AZ 85747
www.azinnovation.com
(520) 382-3260

Presenting Your Business

Creating the elevator pitch, executive summary, investor presentation, and business plan

Investors will want to hear your pitch, read your summary, or be charmed by your presentation. But somewhere along the line, they will still ask to see your business plan. Are you ready? This chapter provides an overview of tools you need to present your business clearly and successfully. It includes traditional and current investor presentation content, resources for business plan development, and a few tips and tricks to help you create your elevator pitch. Elevator included.

The lead contributor is Randy Accetta, Ph.D.,Communications Mentor at the McGuire Center for Entrepreneurship, the University of Arizona. He is also a published author and leading voice for running and fitness. Dr. Accetta has coached hundreds of companies to develop successful investment presentations, and he plays a significant role as a Mentor with the Arizona Center for Innovation.

Presenting Your Business

Randy Accetta

Arizona Center
for Innovation
Office of University Research Parks

Workshop Objectives

The objectives of this workshop are to learn the elements of:

- Elevator pitch
- Executive summary
- Investor presentation
- Business plan

About the Presenter

Randy Accetta, Ph.D.

Run Tucson, LLC

520-991-0733

raccetta2@cox.net

Communications Mentor, McGuire Center for Entrepreneurship

Two-Time Teacher of the Year, Eller College of Management, the University of Arizona

Perspective

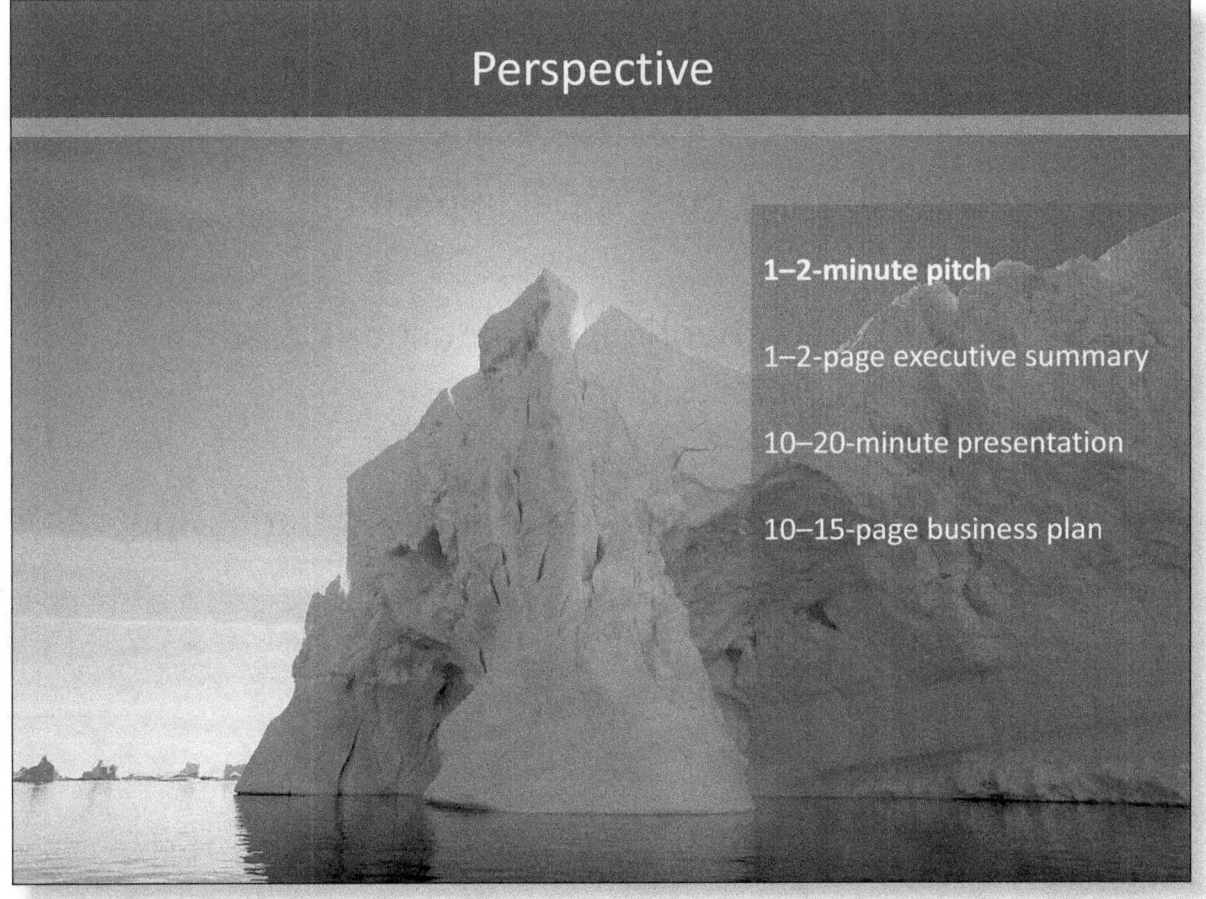

1–2-minute pitch

1–2-page executive summary

10–20-minute presentation

10–15-page business plan

Elevator Pitch

Ability to represent and discuss yourself
- – At any level
- – With anyone
- – At any time . . .

© 2011 Arizona Center for Innovation 5

Elevator Pitch: Duration

1. Ten-second: voice mail, social opportunity

2. Thirty-second: networking introductions, trade shows, social opportunity

3. Two-minute: presentations, interviews, trade shows

© 2011 Arizona Center for Innovation 6

Elevator Pitch: Ways of Looking at It

- An overview of what you do
- Your main communities
- Key benefits to audience
- Primary competitive advantage
- Next steps

Reporter's Questions: Who, What, When, Where, Why?

- Who are you?
- What is the problem or opportunity?
- Who is affected by the problem? Who can benefit from the opportunity?
- What is your solution? How do you solve the problem and add value?
- Where are you - geographically, professionally, metaphorically
- Why you?
- What next?

8 Tips

1. Know your audience

2. Use a hook (story, detail, fact, stat)

3. Give them a reason to remember you

4. Pitch the problem you solve

5. Don't use buzzwords

6. Practice makes perfect

7. Show your superhero strength

8. End with next steps

Remember to be a superhero

- **Remember that you need to show your superhero strength**
  - Are you Superman, able to leap tall buildings?
  - Spiderman, able to send out wonderful webs?
  - Wonder Woman, speedy and smart?

- **What is your venture's superhero competitive advantage?**
  - Valuable intellectual property?
  - First to market?
  - Management team?
  - Cutting-edge technology?

9 Steps

1. Know your audience
2. Keep it simple and tell the truth
3. Image counts
4. Adapt your pitch to the situation
5. How can you add value to the audience?

© 2011 Arizona Center for Innovation 11

9 Steps

6. Be memorable: what is your superhero strength?
7. Differentiate yourself with details
8. Close with a call to action
9. Practice, practice, practice . . .

© 2011 Arizona Center for Innovation 12

Potential Pitch Formula

- **We** *(company, founders)*
- **Have created** *(product, service)*
- **For** *(target customer *numbers are helpful)*
- **Who are dissatisfied with** *(current market alternative).*
- **Our product is** *(new product category).*
- **We provide** *(key problem-solving capability)*
- **Unlike** *(existing alternative).*
- **We have assembled** *(key product features for your specific application).*
- **We want you to . . .**

Source: Modified from Moore, Geoffrey (2002), Crossing the Chasm *(p. 152). New York: HarperCollins.*

Miscellaneous Advice

CLOSE! CLOSE! CLOSE!

Capital need and use

Revenue model

First customer
market opportunity

How YOU solve—WHY better

Problem—solutions

Introduction

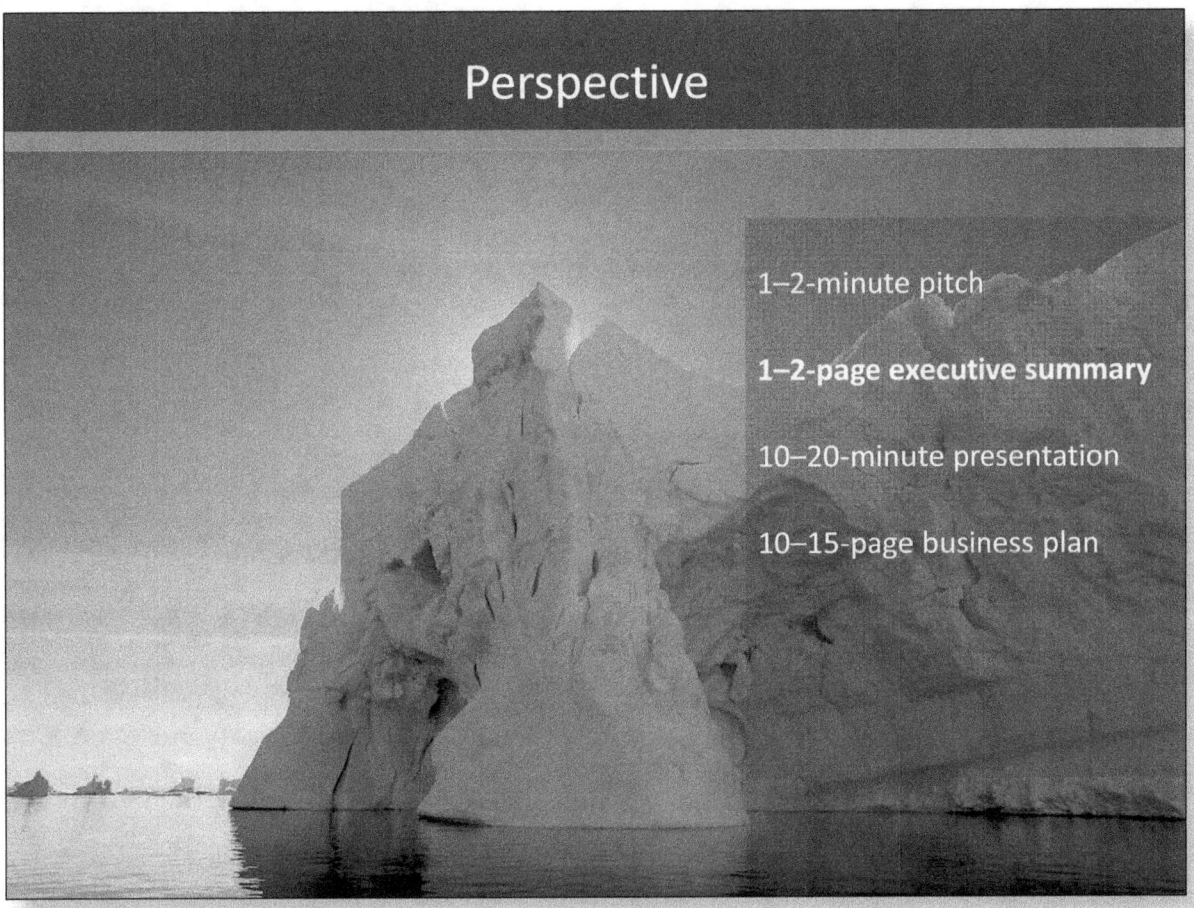

Perspective

1–2-minute pitch

1–2-page executive summary

10–20-minute presentation

10–15-page business plan

The Executive Summary

GOAL

One-page overview of your venture

When do you need two pages?

FOR WHOM? Modify for the audience.

Investors?
Partners?
Customers?
Distributors?
Media?
General marketing?
Mom and dad?

The Executive Summary

Gust.com application:

Desert Angels Example Topics	Characters Allowed
One-line pitch	150
Business summary	450
Management team qualifications	450
Problem	210
Solution	450
Market	450
Current or potential customers	210
Sales and marketing strategy	450
Business model	210
Competitive landscape and competitors	450

Executive Summary, the Gust Way

One-line pitch: 150 characters max, including spaces
Your goal is to summarize your company as succinctly as possible, giving investors and other cultivators a reason to find out more.

Customer problem: 210 characters max, including spaces
What critical customer need does your company address?

Product/services: 450 characters max, including spaces
How does your product solve the customer pain you have described above?

Target market: 450 characters max, including spaces
Define your SPECIFIC market and how it is differentiated from all those impacted by the problem (affected population). Include market size data, growth rate, customer segmentation, and market structure where applicable.

Sales/marketing strategy: 450 characters max, including spaces
How are you going to acquire and maintain customers? Direct sales? Sales representatives or distributors? What is your distribution model? How will customers find you?

Business model: 210 characters max, including spaces
How will you make the value you are creating available, including the transaction?
How do you plan to make money? Are you selling products or services? Are you giving away razors in order to sell razor blades?

Competitors: 450 characters max, including spaces
Every product has competitors (typewriters replaced pencils). What products are your customers now using as painkillers? Who is providing these products to your potential customers? Are these competitors small companies or large public companies?

Competitive Advantage: 210 characters max, including spaces
How will you keep your competitors from quickly copying your products and selling them to your customers? Do you have patents or other proprietary technology? Describe the difficulties your competitors will have in duplicating your solutions.

Financials
Revenue projections 3–5 years. Cash flow statement. Sources and uses of funds.

Team
Management, background, experiences—credibility

Perspective

1–2-minute pitch

1–2-page executive summary

10–20-minute presentation

10–15-page business plan

The Investor Presentation

General guidelines

- Know your audience
- Tell a story—eliminate steps of imagination
- Deliver with and without PowerPoint
- Speak with confidence; you are the expert
- Communicate integrity
- Animate yourself, not your slides—speak conversationally
- Pictures really are worth more
- 10/20/30 rule: 10 slides, 20 minutes, 30-point font
- Practice, practice, practice

Presentation Style

Find a style that's right for you. Here are three examples:

- Traditional: *The Art of the Start*, Guy Kawasaki
- Trend: http://igniteshow.com/
- Personalize: http://www.presentationzen.com/

Find some combination of important facts, story line, and images that reflects your speaking style. Don't forget to include a call to action!

Style: Ignite

http://igniteshow.com/

20 slides each displayed for 15 seconds
Share ideas quickly
Inspire audience to think or act

Ignite is a community hosting events for participants to present a topic of their choice. This is also a great forum to practice your presentation skills.

Style: Presentation Zen

www.presentationzen.com

Focus on images

Tell stories from your own life—you are the presentation

Kawasaki's 10-Slide Rule

Art of the Start, Guy Kawasaki

1. <u>Title</u>: name, contact, mantra
2. <u>Problem</u>: keep it personal
3. <u>Solution</u>: simply how you address problem
4. <u>Business Model</u>: how you make money
5. <u>Underlying Magic</u>: illustrate product, secret sauce
6. <u>Marketing-Sales</u>: generating leads, first customer
7. <u>Competition</u>: landscape of top players
8. <u>Management Team</u>: background, advisors
9. <u>Financials</u>: 5-year projections and key metrics
10. <u>Status</u>: accomplishments, timeline, use of funds

PLUS: Add a SUMMARY slide that recaps value proposition, what you need, and how the audience can make a difference. Include a call to action.

Randy Says: It's You

Devil's in the Details

1. **Introductory Billboard Slide:** Company name, company location, contact information, legal statements (proprietary information, copyright, etc.)
2. **Opening:** Catch attention, describe venture, set stage for pitch
3. **Problem/Opportunity:** The problem your venture will solve, the significance of the problem, the opportunity this offers your venture, quality of the opportunity, growth potential, etc.
4. **Product and/or Service Solution Description:** Essential product/service idea, category of product/service, proprietary protection, entry strategies ...
5. **Customers and Target Markets:** Target market characteristics, size, why this market is the best for your venture, market validation research ...

Devil's in the Details

6. **Business Model:** How your venture will earn a profit, expected margins, sources of recurring revenue ...

7. **Environment and Context:** Industry overview, research results and analysis, major competitors, benchmark ventures, timeliness, regulations ...

8. **Competitive Advantages:** Market focus, value proposition, core competencies, barriers to entry, competitive validation, how your venture will position itself to meet the competition, etc.

9. **Marketing and Sales Strategies:** Pricing strategies, distribution model, partnering, promotional strategies ...

10. **Development Plan:** Current company status, number of employees, development stage, early revenue, number of customers, relevant historical information, long-term venture goals, growth strategies, timeline ...

Devil's in the Details

11. **Operational Strategies:** Production methodologies, manpower requirements, equipment requirements, material management, flow diagram of key processes ...

12. **Intellectual Property and Legal Issues Strategies:** Patents, trademarks, trade names, copyrights, trade secrets, operating and other agreements, legal structure

13. **Organization:** Management team, relevant domain knowledge of the team, commitment, advisors, directors, management to be added, culture, talent ...

14. **Technology Strategies:** Technology, product development ...

15. **Risks and Contingencies:** Downside risks and contingency plans, upside risks and expansion plans ...

Devil's in the Details

16. **Financial Projections:** Key assumptions, historical financial statements, pro forma statements, return on investment ...

17. **Investment Funds Sought, Use of Proceeds, and Harvest Strategy:** Total investment funding being sought, use of funds in 4 or 5 general categories, any unusual use of funds, return of cash to investors and entrepreneurs ...

18. **Summary:** Vision; mission; goals; a brief who, what, where, when, why, and how of your venture ...

19. **Closing:** Creative, memorable, professional—"gets audience to yes." Includes **Closing Billboard Slide**: Company name, company location, contact information ...

20. Variety of **support slides** keyed to most-likely-to-be-asked questions

Handling Q&A

Anticipate questions by creating a Q&A support slide with corresponding backup data. Hyperlink to it, or simply hit numerals-enter on your keyboard.

- Financial details
- Customer testimonials (should also be in your presentation!)
- IP and/or product details
- Anything specific to your venture

Answering Q&A

- Listen, and use questions to drive changes to your presentation for next time.
- Listen, and don't appear defensive or challenged; sometimes people will ask challenging questions just to show how much they know.
- Listen, and if you don't know the answer, offer to follow up.
- Listen, and if they ask about valuation—ask for the close!

Perspective

1–2-minute pitch

1–2-page executive summary

10–20-minute presentation

10–15-page business plan

Purposes of Business Plans

- Create and define strategic plan
- Consolidate research, notes, details, and thoughts
- Organize, engage, and activate your team
- Create vision, focus, and direction for the company, team, and partners
- Mitigate risk
- Generate interest
- Communicate plan to investors, partners, for acquisition

Yes ... investors will want to hear your pitch, read your summary, or be charmed by your presentation. But somewhere along the line they will STILL ask to see your business plan. Are you ready?

Considerations for Your Business Plan

- <u>Stick to the facts</u>: Stay away from negative or inappropriate language and personal comments—let the facts tell your story. Keep it clean and simple, no funny clipart or hard-to-read font.

- <u>Professionalism</u>: Include a title cover page with your company, logo, contact information, and ©; a TOC; footers with page # and your company name. If you are submitting to an investor, include a color cover page and professional binder. Include any marketing collateral or other materials you think appropriate. Track what you send to whom, when.

- <u>Solid armor</u>: Have someone else review and spell-check; the best investors will always look for chinks in your armor to see how well you will execute against your plan. It should reflect and support content in your other presentations.

Considerations for Your Business Plan

- <u>Focus</u>: The business plan is NOT a dumping ground for data; tell a compelling story, target the right audience, and focus on the important points. Make sure your data backs up your story!

- <u>To Outsource or Not</u>: If writing is not your strong suit, you may be inclined to engage the services of someone to help you polish your business plan. This is an important representation of your business, so get trusted referrals and interview your sources carefully. Keep in mind there are no "fast-fix" solutions, and that you still need to do the legwork because no one else will understand your business the way you do.

Business Plan Elements

- Executive summary
- Company description
- Industry analysis and trends
- Target market
- Competition
- Strategic position and risk assessment
- Marketing plan and sales strategy
- Operations
- Technology plan
- Management plan and sales Strategy
- Operations
- Technology plan

- Management and organization
- Community involvement and social responsibility
- Development, milestones, and exit plan
- The financials
- Appendix

Source: *The Successful Business Plan*, Rhonda Abrams

Workshop Summary

This workshop covers the pitch, executive summary, presentation, and plan.

Remember that people want to talk about your business. Help them tell the right facts by creating a pitch they can share. The value of your pitch is not always your ability to deliver ... but for those around you to deliver.

Follow-up:
Schedule a session with your incubator and/or advisor support team and lay out your pitch, summary, presentation, and plan side-by-side for comparison and review. Do you have a compelling story? Can your team deliver your pitch accurately? Have them role-play with you as investors to practice your presentation.

Validating Your Opportunity

Understanding and identifying the problem, your solution, and your first customers

Problem. Solution. Customer. Together they form a loop that requires constant review and validation when bringing a new product or service to market. It's important to understand the problem you are trying to solve and how you will solve it better (your value proposition) and how to make that connection with your first customers. This is an essential part of any company's story and should be a driving factor in building your overall commercialization plan.

The lead contributor is Rick Gibson, Managing Director for HOTventures. Mr. Gibson is a successful serial entrepreneur, investor, and mentor, and serves as Board Member for the Arizona Center for Innovation. Mr. Gibson plays a critical role in the ongoing development, support, growth, and success of the incubator operation and companies.

Problem – Customer – Solution

Presented by Rick Gibson

Office of University Research Parks

www.hotventures.com

Rick Gibson has had a 37-year career immersed in building fast-growth technology companies as an investor, board member, advisor, teacher, judge, screener, public speaker, and writer. He has invested in several companies, participated in dozens, advised a few hundred, and played a key role in a few successful exits. Rick's been actively involved in several incubators, including Silicon Valley's Catalyst Technologies (1980s) and Idealab (late 1990s), currently serving on the boards of UA's AZCI and NAU's NACET. He's active in several Arizona angel groups, and has served on the board of the Desert Angels. He has taught entrepreneurship at UA and ASU. Rick has worked alongside several entrepreneurial icons, including Nolan Bushnell (founder of Atari), and Bill Gross (founder of Idealab) with whom Rick was a cofounder of Knowledge Adventure.

Workshop Objectives

This workshop will help you:

- Define and validate <u>the problem</u> you're trying to solve
- Understand whether or not it presents an opportunity
- Refine and describe <u>your solution</u> and value proposition
- Understand and <u>identify your first customers</u>

The Problem

- Define problem

- True or false
  - All problems require solutions
  - All solutions become opportunities

Formulate the Problem

- Describe the problem
- Does this problem cause discomfort, difficulty, or pain?
- Collect multiple perspectives, look for common ideas

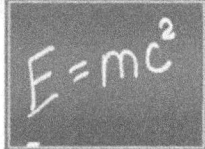

Understand Cause and Impact

- Underlying cause of the problem?
- How is the problem solved today?
- Long-lasting or temporary?
- How BIG is it?
- Is it growing?
- How urgent is the need for a better solution?

Personalize It

- Can you identify with the problem?
- Do you have this problem? Does anyone you know?
- Why do you need a new solution?
- How is the problem perceived by others?
- Can you connect this to your audience?

Interactive Discussion

- Examples of problems ...

Think about simple, common problems that exist today... Kids carrying a heavy load of books to school every day. Battery life of a phone. Something you encountered in the last hour. Can you describe the problem in 25 words or less? Can you think of a simple solution to the problem? Now translate this to your business. Think of the problem you are solving and try to put that in the same kind of simple language. It's not so easy!

Validate the Problem

- Who's affected by this problem and how big is that market?
- Is this a growing population, trend, problem?
- What are problem costs - time, money, health, other? Can you quantify those costs?
- Why does this problem exist?
- Will social, economic, political, or technological trends affect the importance of the problem?
- What else should you be asking?

© 2011 Arizona Center for Innovation 9

Secondary Research

- 1, 2, 3x removed from the source
- Published: online, library, University, etc
- Industry associations, events, trade shows
- Publications
- Trend watch - social listening
- Alternative, competitor, complementary solutions

© 2011 Arizona Center for Innovation 10

Primary Research

- Surveys and questionnaires
- Interviews
- Focus groups
- Prospective customers
- Suppliers, partners, sales channels

TIP: Engage with your customers PERSONALLY and get permission to use their testimonials!

Assess Your Company & Your Competitors

Strengths	Weaknesses
Assets, IP protection, team, partners, expertise, competitive advantages, etc.	Liabilities, lack of assets, no IP protection, missing team players or partners, etc.
Internal: capitalize, promote, and manage your strengths.	Internal: address weaknesses as quickly as possible, fill the gaps.
Opportunities	**Threats**
New distribution channels, complementary products/services, new applications and markets, etc.	Risks, change in regulation, technology obsolescence, change in market interest, distribution, etc.
External: watch for new openings and capture	External: create contingency plans

Research Tips

- DO ...
  - Use reliable sources for information and corroborate
  - Stick to facts: be accurate, realistic
  - Focus on the strengths of your product/service
  - Build credibility by focusing on credible third-party facts

- DON'T ...
  - Take only the first data point
  - Use opinion
  - Say negative things about your competition, partners, market, etc.

> TIP: Keep your notes and resources together in a binder and create a summary of your research. This supplemental data will be important as you pull your business plan together.

© 2011 Arizona Center for Innovation 13

State the Problem

Create a simple problem statement:

- What is the problem?
- How many people are affected?
- What are the trends—is this a growing problem, industry?
- Personalize.

- Keep it simple!

© 2011 Arizona Center for Innovation 14

Pitch on *Gust*

- Consider http://gust.com (210 characters)

Assignment:

Define the problem in 25 words or less

TIP: *"If you can't explain it simply, you don't understand it well enough."*
— *Albert Einstein*

© 2011 Arizona Center for Innovation 15

The Validation Loop

Continuous validation

Problem

Customer

Solution

© 2011 Arizona Center for Innovation 16

Solving the Problem

- How is the problem being handled today?
- How will you address the problem?
- Who else is addressing this problem ... and if the answer is no one, why not?

Is There a Solution?

- Is it practical?
- Do you have the skills to develop?
- Do you have the resources to bring to market?
- What are the risks for your business?
- Is the potential reward worth the risk?
- Can you compete against alternative solutions?
- How is your solution better?

Is There a Business Opportunity?

- Sizeable, reachable, niche market?
- Does that market have wants/needs your solution solves?
- What benefits does your solution offer?
- Options for expansion, diversification, integration? Growth?

- What is your value proposition?
  Value = Benefits - Price

Is the Business Model Sustainable?

Will your solution make money?

- Profit = Revenue - Expenses
- Profit margin should be durable regardless of changing technology, customer preferences, personnel or company change, partner or distributor changes, etc.

What About the Competition?

- How do they address this problem?
- Will your solution displace theirs?
- How will they respond?
- What are their strengths and weaknesses?

> TIP: Understanding your competitors may help you better understand the market, identify trends and changes, spark new ideas, and better define your OWN company strengths. These competitors may become a benchmark for your growth, and how you choose to position your company in the market. Keep these notes in your research binder, and this should be an ongoing review … even after your company dominates the market!

Validate … Again

- Primary and secondary research
- SWOT analysis
- Keep notes
- Do: use reliable sources and stick to facts
- Don't: take only one data point or use opinion

> TIP: Engage with your customers PERSONALLY and get permission to use their testimonials!

Differentiation Is Important

- Have a unique selling proposition
- Have a <u>competitive advantage</u>
- Do something that no other business does, and in a way that no other business can easily duplicate

Present Your Solution

Restate the problem

- Describe how YOU solve the problem
- Describe how you solve the problem BETTER
- Keep it simple
- Keep it personal

> Tip: As you create your problem and solution statement, think about how this will fit into your company pitch. You'll want to describe the problem and who is affected, the size of the opportunity, and how you solve it (better).

State the Problem/Solution in 50 Words

- Less is more, but harder!
- You need more to have less
- Consider http://gust.com , 450 characters

Assignment:

Restate the problem and
define your solution.

Can you do both in under
50 words?

Customer

Identify your <u>Potential</u> Customer

- Who has this problem?
- What are they doing now?
- Is the problem considered urgent?

- Why would someone switch from the current solution to your solution?

Identify Your <u>Target</u> Customer

- Who uses the solution?
- Who chooses the solution?
- Who pays for the solution?
- Who benefits from the solution?

- They may be different, but all have a stake.

Example: Medical Diagnostic Tests

- Who uses the solution? Lab technician
- Who chooses the solution? Doctor
- Who pays for the solution? Insurer (sometimes patient)
- Who benefits from the solution? All of the above

Example: Home Automation Hardware

- Who uses the solution? The home owner
- Who chooses the solution? Installer
- Who pays for the solution? Home builder
- Who benefits from the solution? All of the above

Identify Your Customer

For your business ...

- Who uses the solution?
- Who chooses the solution?
- Who pays for the solution?
- Who benefits from the solution?

- Understanding the WHO helps you identify your first customers and how they may actually buy your product. You'll also want to go to each partner to identify different issues and/or needs.

The Buying Decision

Does your solution:

- Solve the problem?
- Improve quality of life through time saving or other perceived issues?
- Provide financial benefits: is it affordable, can your customer afford to switch, are there hidden or long-term ownership costs?

Not Selling ... It's Buying!

Does your solution:

- Offer convenience: easy to adopt, easy to use?
- Provide emotional benefits: fill a need, affect self-image, social significance?

> TIP: People do not like to be sold anything. They like to buy. The difference between the two is CHOICE. Remember that this is a WIN-WIN situation; you are helping them solve their problem in a new/better way. Understanding WHO the decision maker is, and HOW they are motivated to buy, can make all the difference.

Dos/Don'ts

DO

"Our first five target customers are: Best Buy, Radio Shack, Ace Hardware, Home Depot, and Lowe's. We have a letter of intent from Mr X at the new Ace Hardware on Houghton Road to buy 500 of our units by next month."

DON'T

"We plan to capture just 1% of a $100 billion market."

Market vs. Customer

Invest in building close customer relationships from the start.

- Bringing customers in early (where appropriate) leads to great feedback, testimonials, partnerships, promotions, and possibly sales! And of course, *credibility*.

- The further along you are in this process, the stronger your traction, the more value you build, and the more likely you are to attract partners and investors.

Focus on Your First Customers

Assignment:

Identify your top 10 customers. When ready, invite each to participate in a brainstorm session to learn more about their needs and solicit feedback on your ideas.

Again ... Validate

Recap

- Define and validate the problem you are trying to solve and understand whether or not it presents an opportunity
- Refine and describe your solution and value proposition
- Understand and identify your first customers

For Discussion

1. What factors create the opportunity potential of your problem?
2. How important is the problem to you and why?
3. Who are the users, customers, and payers for your solution?
4. What is the value proposition of your solution?
5. How does your solution create a viable business?
6. What are the buying influences of your customers?
7. Why would customers want your solution?
8. Articulate the problem and your solution.

Moving Forward

Take the next steps:

- Talk with your incubator staff and mentors to get inspired and ask for help.
- Work on the assignment.
- Think about your pitch—this assignment is the start of something big!

Congratulations!

Assignment:

Simply state the problem and define your solution (and how it's better) in 50 words or less. Practice makes perfect; get others to repeat.

Identify and talk with your top 10 customers.

Safeguarding Your Ideas

Identifying, protecting, and defending your intellectual property

Intellectual property (IP) plays a critical role in the development and planning for any new technology venture, especially when it comes to finding the right strategy to identify, protect, and defend that IP. The purpose of this session is to help participants navigate through four key areas: patents, trade secrets, trademark, and copyrights; it also addresses the importance of avoiding infringement of others' IP. In addition, the presentation includes a few tips and resources for conducting a patent or trademark search.

This chapter is presented by Snell & Wilmer LLP, a full-service business law firm with more than 400 attorneys practicing in nine locations throughout the western United States and Mexico. Snell & Wilmer LLP is a valued mentor and partner with the Arizona Center for Innovation and has served many start-up ventures in our community.

Getting Off to a Good Start:
Strategies for Startup Companies to Identify, Protect, and Defend Their Intellectual Property

Presented by Snell & Wilmer LLP

Office of University Research Parks

Snell & Wilmer LLP

Began in Phoenix in 1938 and has grown to be the largest law firm in Arizona

Over 400 attorneys in 9 offices:
- Denver   - Orange County
- Las Vegas   - Phoenix
- Los Angeles   - Reno
- Los Cabos   - Salt Lake City
- Tucson

30+ intellectual property attorneys

"Hybrid" intellectual property practice

Prepared by Snell & Wilmer LLP, for the Arizona Center for Innovation 2

Cynthia Pillote, Partner, Intellectual Property Group

Cindy's practice focuses on working with clients to develop, implement, and manage business strategies for procuring, maintaining, and enforcing intellectual property rights. Her practice includes US and foreign patent, trademark, and copyright prosecution; patent due diligence; technology transfer and licensing; and business transactions. Cynthia's technical experience has primarily focused on nanotechnology, semiconductors, and semiconductor manufacturing, medical devices and products, organic and inorganic chemistry compounds and processes, pharmaceuticals, life sciences, cosmeceuticals, electronic commerce, mechanical devices, mining technology, green technology, and electronic communication.

William Mulholland, II, Counsel, Intellectual Property Group

Bill's practice is concentrated in intellectual property law, including patent, copyright, and trademark licensing, litigation, and procurement. His past experience includes serving as in-house counsel for pharmaceutical and agribusiness-based industries. A substantial portion of Bill's practice involves strategic counseling for these industries, including all IP-related aspects of discovery, development, and commercialization activities. Bill has extensive transactional experience and has successfully negotiated a wide range of licenses and other agreements in support of various industry and university alliances. His patent procurement practice includes comprehensive life-cycle management planning, from emerging technologies to post-patent expiry of commercial products. Bill's life sciences practice includes small molecule chemistry and biologic therapeutics, as well as diagnostics, drug discovery, and drug delivery. His agribusiness practice similarly focuses on chemical and biologic-based active ingredients, as well as formulation and chemical process technologies. Bill's practice also includes US interferences and European oppositions as well as matters before the USPTO Board of Appeals and the federal courts. Prior to joining Snell & Wilmer, Bill was part of a litigation team that obtained a patent infringement jury verdict of $49 million and findings of noninfringement on multiple patent claims brought by the defendant.

Snell & Wilmer LLP

Eric Nielsen, Associate, Intellectual Property Group

Eric's practice is centered on intellectual property counseling; in particular, the design and implementation of business-driven strategies to identify, protect, defend, enforce, and otherwise build value in IP assets, including patents, trademarks, copyrights, and trade secrets. He has experience in virtually all facets of IP law including patent and trademark prosecution (US and foreign), proceedings before the Board of Patent Appeals and Interferences and the Trademark Trial and Appeal Board, clearance searching and invalidity and noninfringement opinion work, patentability searching and trademark screening, IP dispute resolution and litigation, IP licensing, and other diverse agreements and business transactions having IP components. Eric has worked with clients ranging from sole inventors, emerging growth companies, and those seeking angel investing and venture capital to Fortune 500 companies, and he has technical expertise in, among other fields, bioengineering, medical devices, pharmaceuticals, mechanical devices, "green" technologies, nanotechnology, and a variety of consumer products and business methods. Eric regularly presents on various IP topics and is currently a member of Snell & Wilmer's Summer Associate Committee.

Workshop Objectives

Provide participants with an intellectual property overview

Discuss types of intellectual property
- — Patents
- — Trade secrets
- — Trademarks
- — Copyrights

Create a plan to identify and protect your intellectual property

Avoid the thicket of third-party IP

Workshop Objectives

Enable you to add value to your company by:

- Identifying your intellectual property
- Protecting your valuable intellectual property
- Steering clear of third-party intellectual property

What is Intellectual Property?

Intellectual property includes tangible and intangible ideas, information, and things that are created or derived and that have a commercial value.

Intellectual property rights are bestowed on the owners of ideas, inventions, and creative expression that have the status of property, and like tangible property, <u>gives the owner the right to exclude others from access to or use of their property.</u>

What Can I Do with My Intellectual Property?

Offensive tool: prevent others from using
- Sue for damages
- Injunctions
- Ownership alone is often a deterrent

Defensive tool: if someone tries to prevent you from doing something
- Prevent others from monopolizing
- Set up motivation for cross licensing

Corporate Asset
- Sell or license
- Leverage to: cross-license, create partnerships

Prepared by Snell & Wilmer LLP, for the Arizona Center for Innovation 9

Intellectual Property Assets

COMPONENTS OF S&P 500 MARKET VALUE

	1975	1985	1995	2005	2010
Tangible Assets	83%	68%	32%	20%	20%
Intangible Assets	17%	32%	68%	80%	80%

☐ TANGIBLE ASSETS ▨ INTANGIBLE ASSETS

Source: Ocean Tomo

10

Why Is IP Important to a Startup?

- Exclusive rights are often required to procure investment in technology to bring products and/or services to market

- Often the only equity value a startup has to show investors

- Understanding others' IP is important:
  - Helps define your rights
  - May mitigate likelihood of threats from others
  - Helps you and your investors understand the value of your IP

Intellectual Property Overview

Four main areas of intellectual property:

1. Patents
2. Trade secrets
3. Trademarks
4. Copyrights

1. Patents

Rights: a legal right to exclude others from making, using, selling, or offering to sell a patented invention (not a right to make, use, sell, or offer to sell)

Policy: advance innovation through disclosure and teaching of details of the invention to the public in exchange for exclusive rights for a term

To qualify, an invention must be:
- Useful
- Novel
- Nonobvious
- The specification must also contain a written description of the invention, and of the manner and process of making and using it, in such full, clear, concise, and exact terms as to enable any person skilled in the art to which it pertains, or with which it is most nearly connected, to make and use the same, and shall set forth the best mode contemplated by the inventor of carrying out his invention

1. Patents

What is patentable?
- "Anything under the sun that is made by man"
- Machines and devices
- Processes (e.g., to make materials or use materials, machines or, devices)
- Methods of manufacture (e.g., to make machines, devices, or compositions of matter)
- Composition of matter (e.g., pharmaceutical compounds)
- Business methods
- Designs
- Plants

What is not patentable: discoveries, ideas, theories

Term:
- Effective as of the issue date, not before
- 20 years from earliest claimed priority date (typically ~17 years from issuance)

2. Trade Secrets

Definition: a trade secret generally means information, including a formula, pattern, compilation, program, device, method, technique, or process, that both:

— derives independent economic value, actual or potential, from not being generally known to, and not being readily ascertainable by proper means by, other persons who can obtain economic value from its disclosure or use;

— is the subject of efforts that are reasonable under the circumstances to maintain its secrecy

Need not be completely novel or exclusive, but must have a derived or potential economic value from being unknown.

2. Trade Secrets

Rights
— A trade secret's owner has the right to prevent the unauthorized use or disclosure of trade secret information by a person who acquired the information through improper means
— No rights against a person who acquires the purported secret through other means—e.g., inspection, reverse engineering, publications
— No rights against a person who independently creates the information

Term
— As long as the owner successfully prevents the trade secret from becoming widely known

2. Trade Secrets

What is protectable using trade secret rights?

- Compositions
- Processes to make compositions
  - Specific conditions such as temperature, pressure
  - Specific chemicals and/or the corresponding suppliers
- Devices used to manufacture compositions or devices
- Potential or actual customers

3. Trademarks

Definition: any word, name, symbol, or device, or any combination thereof
- (1) used by a person, or
- (2) which a person has a bona fide intention to use in commerce
- which is used to identify and distinguish his or her goods, including a unique product, from those manufactured or sold by others and to indicate the source of the goods, even if that source is unknown

Policy: prevent the public from being misled as to the origin or quality of a product or service

3. Trademarks

Common law trademark protection

- Based on first use of a trademark in a particular territory
- Territory: protection is limited to geographic area in which trademark-bearing goods sold—allows other TM owners to use same mark in remote areas
- TM/SM: Any time you claim rights in a mark, you may and should use the "TM" (trademark) or "SM" (service mark) designation to alert the public to your claim of rights

3. Trademarks

Federally registered trademark protection

- Must file an application and obtain registration
- Territory: countrywide
- Benefits received through federal registration include:
  - Constructive notice to the public of the registrant's claim of ownership of the mark
  - A legal presumption of the registrant's ownership of the mark and the registrant's exclusive right to use the mark nationwide on or in connection with the goods and/or services listed in the registration
  - The use of the US registration as a basis to obtain registration in foreign countries
  - The ability to file the US registration with the US Customs Service to prevent importation of infringing foreign goods

- Common law trademark ™
- Registered trademark ®

3. Trademarks

Rights

- Right to prevent others from using the same or similar mark in any way that creates a likelihood of confusion as to the source of the respective goods or services

Term

- For so long as the mark is used on or in connection with goods or services
- Federal registrations require registration renewal

3. Trademarks

What might be protectable using trademark rights?

- Goodwill associated with manufacturer or seller of goods or services
- Same or similar marks on same or similar goods

4. Copyrights

Copyrightable material: any original works of authorship fixed in a tangible medium of expression, such as:
- Software
- Books
- Paintings
- This presentation!

General requirements
- Original. This means "not copied." The work need not be completely original, but may not be merely a trivial variation of another work
- Works of authorship. This requirement excludes ideas, procedures, processes, systems, methods of operation, concepts, principles, discoveries, or facts
- Fixed in a tangible medium of expression. A piece of paper, a stone tablet, a CD, a computer hard disk, or even computer memory

Policy: encourage the expression of original, artistic ideas into a tangible medium

4. Copyrights

Rights:
- To make and distribute copies
- To make derivative works
- To publicly perform or display the work

Fair Use:
- Allows reproduction for limited purposes such as criticism, comment, news reporting, teaching, and research

Term:
- Copyright in a work created on or after January 1, 1978, subsists from its creation and, except as provided by the following subsections, endures for a term consisting of the life of the author and 70 years after the author's death.
- In the case of an anonymous work, a pseudonymous work, or a work made for hire, the copyright endures for a term of 95 years from the year of its first publication, or a term of 120 years from the year of its creation.

4. Copyrights

What might be protectable using copyrights?

- Instructions
- Diagrams
- Pictures
- Papers
- Presentations
- Website content
- Computer programs

© 2011 Author Name

Building a Competitive Advantage

Positioning your company for success

A competitive advantage exists when you have something that your customers consider to be *better* than the competition. Those advantages may include unique intellectual property, better features, easier access, lower prices, etc. The presentation discusses competitive advantage and provides a model to help you position your company in the market.

The lead contributor is Jim Butler, CEO and Founder of HJ3. He is a successful entrepreneur, and in 2008 he was inducted in to the University of Arizona Entrepreneurship Hall of Fame. He is a Mentor for the Arizona Center for Innovation, providing advice and guidance for new entrepreneurs.

Building Your
Competitive Advantage

Presented by Jim Butler

Arizona Center for Innovation
Office of University Research Parks

About the Presenter

Jim Butler, CEO and Founder, HJ3

In 2007 Mr. Butler was named as one of Tucson's "40-Under-40" by the *Arizona Daily Star*. In 2008 he was inducted in to the University of Arizona Entrepreneurship Hall of Fame. He holds an MBA in entrepreneurship and finance from the University of Arizona.

Workshop Objectives

- Define competitive advantage

- Understand and recognize key competitive advantages, and the value of a sustainable competitive advantage

- Use Michael Porter's 5-Forces Model to position your company against the bargaining power of suppliers and buyers, threat of new entrants, industry competitors, intensity of rivalry, and substitute products and services

What Is a Competitive Advantage?

A competitive advantage exists when a firm has a product or service perceived by its target market customers as better than that of its competitors. This allows the firm to sustain profits that exceed the average for its industry

2 Myths Surrounding Competitive Advantage

Entrepreneurs are confronted with 2 myths surrounding the creation of a competitive advantage:

1. Most good business opportunities are already gone

2. Small firms cannot compete as well as big companies

Flaws that Plague Entrepreneurs' Thinking

- Imitate Rivals - possess no true competitive advantage
- Susceptible to imitation - competitive advantage is not sustainable
- Misreading the attractiveness of an industry - may not be the fastest growing or most glamorous

Creating a Competitive Advantage

To create a competitive advantage, a firm must have resources and capabilities that are superior to those of its competitors

Creating a Competitive Advantage

Key Resources—the firm's specific assets

- Patents & trademarks
- Know-how
- Reputation & brand equity
- Installed customer base
- Advantage through geography

Capabilities - the firm's ability to utilize its resources

- Ex: Ability to bring products to market faster than competitors
- "Good to Great": Right people on the bus, sitting in the right seats. Disciplined culture; the entire company is focused only on what they can be the best in the world at.

Creating a Competitive Advantage

Cost advantage
- Deliver the same benefits as competitors but at a lower cost
- Examples: Ikea, Costco, Walmart

Differentiation advantage
- Deliver benefits that exceed those of competing products
- Example: Apple Computer

A Model of Competitive Advantage

Resources → Distinctive Competencies ← Capabilities → Cost advantage or Differentiation Advantage → Value Creation

Positioning Your Firm—Step by Step

1. Analyze the industry using Porter's 5-Forces Model to determine the competitive pressures that exist in your industry.
2. Analyze and rank your firm against your competitors. How are you weaker or stronger than them?
3. Determine what your resources are and what your unique capabilities are that allow you to create distinct competencies.
4. What type of competitive advantage do you have: Cost or Performance?
5. How must you position yourself in the market to leverage your competitive advantage?

Determine Competitive Pressure in Your Industry

The more completely entrepreneurs understand the forces of competitive pressure, the better they will be able to assess opportunities and threats facing their venture - **and properly position their company!**

Porter's 5-Forces Model

Porter's 5 Market Forces

Evaluate the competitive pressures in an industry to determine how a firm must position itself to be successful

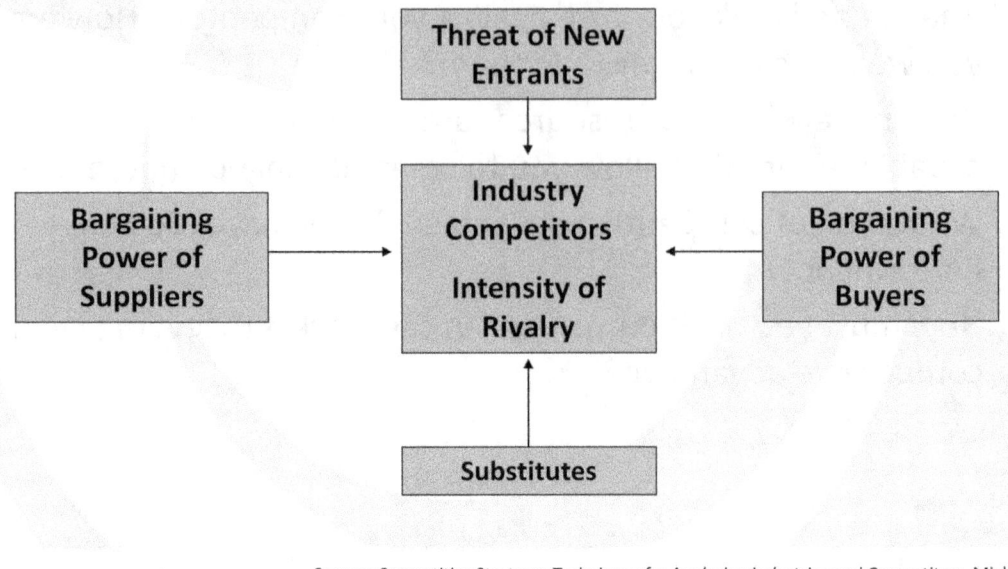

Source: *Competitive Strategy: Techniques for Analyzing Industries and Competitors*, Michael Porter

Intensity of Rivalry

Influences prices as well as costs of competing with rivals in areas such as product development, sales, and advertising

High intensity of Rivalry among competitors is determined by ...

- There are many players similar in size
- Players have similar strategies
- There is not much differentiation between players and their products or services
- Profitability is low for every single company in the industry

Competition erodes profits and creates commodities—oil, sugar, etc.

Source: *Competitive Strategy: Techniques for Analyzing Industries and Competitors*, Michael Porter

Analyze Your Competitors

- Create a comparison grid to see how you stack up against the competition. List those features/details that you think are important to your customers. (1=Best; 4=Worst)
- Use this to identify key areas of differentiation: "I am the best in class/reliable alternative … how do I translate that to sales?"

	YOU	Co A	Co B	Co C
Sales	2M	4M	10M	7M
Price	4	3	1	2
Packaging	4	1	3	2
Quality	1	3	4	2
Client Fulfillment	1	2	3	2

Bargaining Power of Suppliers

Determines the cost of raw materials and other inputs

High Bargaining Power of Suppliers occurs when …

- Market is dominated by a few large suppliers
- There are no substitutes for the particular input
- Supplier's customers are fragmented, so their bargaining power is low
- The switching costs from one supplier to another are high
- There is the possibility of the supplier integrating forward in order to obtain higher prices and margins.

Source: *Competitive Strategy: Techniques for Analyzing Industries and Competitors*, Michael Porter

Bargaining Power of Buyers

Influences the prices that firms can charge as well as the cost and investment required to service buyers

Higher Bargaining Power of Buyers (customers) when ...

- There is a concentration of buyers that buy large volumes
- The supplying industry comprises a large number of small operators
- The product has plenty of substitutes
- Switching to an alternative product is relatively simple and is not related to higher costs
- The customer knows about the production costs of the product
- There is a possibility of the customer integrating backward

Source: *Competitive Strategy: Techniques for Analyzing Industries and Competitors*, Michael Porter

The Threat of New Entrants

Places a limit on prices and shapes the investment required to deter entrants

Threat of New Entrants will depend on barriers to entry ...

- Economies of scale
- Brand loyalty
- IP: patents, trade secrets, & know-how
- High up-front capital requirements
- Access to raw material &/or distribution channels are controlled by existing players
- High switching costs for customers
- Legislation and government action

Source: *Competitive Strategy: Techniques for Analyzing Industries and Competitors*, Michael Porter

Threat of Substitutes

The threat of substitutes exists if there are alternative products with better prices or better performance for the same purpose

The Threat of Substitutes are determined by factors like ...

- Brand loyalty of customers
- Close customer relationships
- Switching costs for customers
- Relative price for performance of substitutes

Source: *Competitive Strategy: Techniques for Analyzing Industries and Competitors*, Michael Porter

Apple Computer—Porter's 5 Forces

	PC Market	Online Music/Apps	Mobile Devices
Threat of Entry	Low High capital requirements High brand loyalty IP	Low High capital requirements High brand loyalty IP	Low High capital requirements High brand loyalty IP
Intensity of Rivalry	Low Few large players Very different strategies High differentiation	Low Few large players Very different strategies High differentiation	High Few large players More Imitation Minimal differentiation
Threat of Substitutes	Low High brand loyalty Can charge premium for product differentiation High switching costs	Low High switching costs Integration with player Close customer relationships	Moderate Imitation higher Phones sold through cell phone plans Some brand loyalty
Power of Suppliers	Low Self-reliant Integration	Moderate Content providers high Self-reliant on software & CE	Low Wireless providers high Self-reliant on software & CE
Power of Buyers	Moderate Low concentration of buyers Few suppliers Moderate switching costs	Low Low concentration of buyers Few suppliers High switching costs	Moderate Low concentration of buyers Few suppliers Moderate switching costs

Compare to Competitors

PC Market	Apple	HP	Dell	Lenovo
Price	4	3	2	1
Quality	1	3	2	4
Hip Features	1	3	2	4
Quality	1	2	3	4
Client Fulfillment	1	3	2	4

A Model of Competitive Advantage - Apple

Resources
Brand equity
Installed customer base
Self-reliant design team

Distinctive Competencies
Best-in-class products
Supported by most
loyal client base

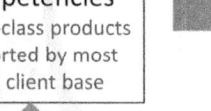

Cost Advantage or Differentiation Advantage

Value Creation

Capabilities
Continual innovation
Rapid product launch
Hip products designed with
the user in mind!

"Apple is operating its own closed miniature techno-economy … they produce everything themselves: their own hardware, software, operating systems, search engines, and consumer electronics to an adoring client base who can't get enough"
Technology review for *Time Magazine*, Lev Grossman

Positioning Your Firm—Step by Step

1. Analyze the industry using the Porter analysis to determine the competitive pressures that exist in your industry

2. Analyze and compare your firm to your competitors. How are you weaker or stronger than them?

3. Determine what your resources are and what your unique capabilities are that allow you to create distinct competencies?

4. What type of competitive advantage do you have? Cost or Differentiation?

5. How must you position yourself in the market to leverage your competitive advantage and make it sustainable?

Summary

- A competitive advantage exists when a firm has a product or service perceived by its target market customers as better than that of its competitors. This allows the firm to sustain profits that exceed the average for its industry.

- Use Michael Porter's 5-Forces Model to position your company against the bargaining power of suppliers and buyers, threat of new entrants, industry competitors, intensity of rivalry, and substitute products and services.

Things to Keep in Mind

- How will you know how to position your product?
  - Based on market research and consumer preferences, adjust product design, delivery accordingly
  - Map product characteristics to consumer preferences, not the other way around
- How do I avoid imitation and sustain my competitive advantage?
  - Who are the competitors, and do they have the resources or capabilities to imitate our offering
  - Can I put resources towards barriers to entry
    - Patents, Trademarks, Copyrights
    - High Switching Cost (Customer Loyalty Programs, Exclusive Distributor Agreements, Unwavering Customer Service)

Exploring Your Market

Primary and secondary market research

Creating a new venture? Launching a new product or service? Trying to reach a new market? Need to know what's happening in the industry? Want to learn more about your customers and why they are or are not buying? Market research is not a one-time-project required for your business plan. Instead, consider it an ongoing journey of discovery. It sets the course for your new venture but will also provide guidance and direction when you may need it most. This chapter introduces the concepts of primary versus secondary market research; provides an in-depth look at various market research strategies and resources, and even includes a few tips and ideas for follow-up.

The lead contributor is Jan Knight, President of Bancroft Information Services, LLC. Ms. Knight is a leading expert in market research; she is the go-to resource for many other marketing firms and has been a valuable partner and mentor for many incubator companies that have gone on to great successes.

Market Research

Presented by Jan Knight
Bancroft Information Services, LLC

Business & Market Research
Information for the Competitive Edge

Office of University Research Parks

About the Presenter

Jan Knight,

Bancroft Information Services, LLC

Jan Knight is an independent business/market researcher whose research often helps to shape business plans, marketing plans, and business development. Her clients range from start-ups to established companies in a variety of industries.

Business & Market Research
Information for the Competitive Edge

www.bancroftinfo.com

jan@bancroftinfo.com

520-731-9300

Prepared for Arizona Center for Innovation 2011, P2

Objectives—What We'll Cover

- Market research
  - "Primary" vs "secondary"
- Market research planning & strategies
- Primary research
- Secondary market research
  - Strategies
  - Sources
  - Tips for research

Market Research

Gathering, recording, and analyzing information about your business.
Make better-informed decisions. Research matters!

- Business plans, marketing plans, product development, looking for funding
- *Industry information:* key players, segmentation, statistics, trends
- *Competitors:* services & products, sales methods, marketing, distribution
- *Market potential:* statistics, demographics, market drivers
- Executive and company searching

Primary Research

- Data collected from original source
- Collected for a specific purpose—*i.e., determine if current customers are happy with a service.*

- *Qualitative* (focus groups, interviews): Not based on measurable input. Opinions are not projectable to larger population
- *Quantitative* (surveys): Hard facts or opinions representative and projectable to larger population

Traditional or with emerging technologies: Mobile Phones, Web surveys, Online Focus Groups

Prepared for Arizona Center for Innovation 2011, P5

Primary Research: Focus Groups

- **Pros:** Homogeneous group, spontaneous input, can be redirected, stimulate new ideas, need a good moderator to stimulate interaction
- **Cons:** Recruiting issues, small sample, cannot generalize to larger population, validity considerations, incentives

- **Example story:** Medical device prototype
  It would have been too big for nurses' hands had they not conducted a focus group

Prepared for Arizona Center for Innovation 2011, P6

Primary Research: Surveys

- **Mail surveys**: affords longer, complicated questions, shows product in picture
- **Phone surveys**: can control sample (respondents)
- **Email surveys**: quick turnaround, less expensive
- NOW ... web and mobile surveys

BUT on all surveys ...

- Response rate can be low & slow
- Need good list to select from
- Often cannot show product
- Little control over who responds

Prepared for Arizona Center for Innovation 2011, P7

Secondary Research

- Also known as "desk" research—UK & Europe
- Accessing of information & data previously collected
- Often for different purpose
- Good precursor to primary research
- Provides a picture of what's happening nationally or internationally
- Identifies trends and provides context

  (articles, studies, newspapers, company databases)

  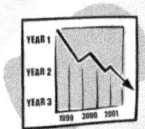

Prepared for Arizona Center for Innovation 2011, P8

Factors Determining Costs

Secondary:
- Mature industries have more information
- New & niche industries not studied as much = less information
- Less expensive than primary research
- BUT robust data requires $ ... usually fee-based databases
- Turnaround time

Primary
- Focus groups: # of groups & locations
- Cost of incentives for focus group participants
- Interviews: # and location of in-depth personal interviews (IDIs)
- Surveys: # of questions & respondents
- Writing of questions
- Type of analysis, tabulations, and reporting needed

Prepared for Arizona Center for Innovation 2011, P9

Search Strategies: Secondary Research

Assess potential availability of information
- Who else would have commissioned a study on what you want to know?
- Who has money to pay for such studies?
- Where would articles or results have been published?
- What conferences would focus on the topic?
- Who are the experts on the subject/industry who might write about and cite the research—industry analysts, authors, journalists.

Think about your own industry and specific sources!

Prepared for Arizona Center for Innovation 2011, P10

Sources: Subscription Databases

Subscription fee-based online databases ($$$$)

- Lexis Nexis: www.lexisnexis.com
- Factiva: www.factiva.com
- Dialog: www.dialog.com
- Hoovers: www.hoovers.com (hybrid—some free, some $)
- IBISWorld: www.ibisworld.com
- Plunkett: www.plunkettresearch.com
- And many more used by information professionals and librarians

- Thousands of sources, information on companies, industries, demographics, national & international.

Prepared for Arizona Center for Innovation 2011, P11

Search Strategies—Internet & More

- What do you know already?
- Know your goal—what info gaps do you need to fill?
- Create source list—"Don't just Google it!"
- Use tools, not just search engines
- Review keywords and phrases
- Document sources & keywords used
- Talk to experts
- Know when to stop!

Prepared for Arizona Center for Innovation 2011, P12

Try These Phrases

Market research reports often have common headings:

- Market share
- Market data
- Industry profile
- Industry trends
- Best practices
- Market trends
- Customer demographics
- Benchmarking
- Best practices

- Consumer preferences
- Growth trends
- Lessons learned
- Competitive landscape
- Commercialization
- Go to market strategy
- White papers
- Polls, studies, surveys
- Statistics

Prepared for Arizona Center for Innovation 2011, P13

Sources: Market Research Reports

- Fee based—often expensive
- Some companies are generalists, others focus on an industry
- Occasionally provide free sample abstracts
- Variations in data based on differences in methodology
- Some companies sell pieces "by the slice"

Finding market research reports:
- MarketResearch.com: www.marketresearch.com (aggregator)
- Gartner Research: www.gartner.com
- Forrester Research: www.forrester.com
- AC Nielsen: www.acnielsen.com
- Frost & Sullivan: www.frost.com

Prepared for Arizona Center for Innovation 2011, P14

Sources: Newspapers & Business Mags

- Look for local stories on competitors, potential vendors, potential clients. People open up when being featured in the news.
- *"Big fish in little pond"* vs. *"little fish in big pond."* **Phoenix Business Journal** versus **New York Times.**
- Small private companies likely to get local attention.

Finding Newspapers and News:

- Online newspapers: www.onlinenewspapers.com/
- Business journals: http://www.bizjournals.com/
- Google News: http://news.google.com/

Sources: Industry & Trade Associations

- Membership of professionals in a field
- Often commission studies and share/sell results
- Specific member benefits may include access to member lists, data on members, ability to e-mail members a survey
- Do they have a trade journal?
- Do your target markets belong to associations?
- Do you belong to a trade association?

Finding trade associations:

- Internet public library associations: www.ipl.org
- Marketing source: www.marketingsource.com/associations/

Sources: Trade Shows/Conferences

- Look at online program
- Who is speaking - experts?
- Look at topics - can you discern trends or issues of importance?
- Review Exhibitor & Sponsor lists
- "Hang out where your (*clients, customers, competitors, partners, collaborators, etc.*) hang out!"

Finding trade shows:

- Trade Show News Network: www.tsnn.com (search by topic, city, industry, dates)

Prepared for Arizona Center for Innovation 2011, P17

Sources: Blogs & Social Media

- Blogs, Facebook, Twitter, LinkedIn
- Caution: Who is posting and why? Real reviews?
  - *"Only 4% of unhappy customers will provide feedback on a survey, while 52% of buyers will likely post a product review on a blog or online forum."* – Quirks Market Research.
  - Can include good, solid customer feedback
  - Look for business pages or connections on Facebook and LinkedIn

Finding blogs:

- Google blog search: www.google.com/blogsearch
- Technorati: www.technorati.com
- Blog Search Engine: http://www.blogsearchengine.com/

Prepared for Arizona Center for Innovation 2011, P18

Sources: Government Websites

- Authoritative
- Timely
- Robust data—sometimes have to dig (Census)
- Examples of data: census, people/economic, trade, demographics, labor statistics, international trade

Finding government information:

- Bureau of Labor Statistics: www.bls.gov
- First Gov: www.firstgov.gov
- Department of the US Census: www.census.gov
- Google government sites: www.google.com/unclesam

Sources: Wikipedia

Q. **Can you really trust Wikipedia?**

A. **Not really, but you can use it wisely**.

WIKIPEDIA
The Free Encyclopedia

- Community-based—anyone can edit
- Use only as primer & starting point
- Review resources/citations
- Corroborate with other sources
- Do NOT cite as source (especially to VCs or funders)

www.wikipedia.org

Company Information

Why do you need?

- Potential clients or customers
- Potential collaborators/partners/funders
- Competitors

Public (easier to find information)
- – Full disclosure
- – SEC (Securities and Exchange Commission) filings
- – Annual reports, quarterly reports
- – Agreements with employees/vendors

Private (harder-to-find information, but often can for fee)
- – Not forced to disclose anything, other than to IRS

Prepared for Arizona Center for Innovation 2011, P21

Company Websites

- Search for PPT (PowerPoint presentations)
- Press releases
- Annual reports
- Biographical info on executives
- History of company - product development
- Branding/differentiation
- Look at employment opportunities - shows plans for future
- Marketing strategies
- Sales/distribution channels

Caution—they tell you what they want you to know!

Prepared for Arizona Center for Innovation 2011, P22

TIP: Use Advanced Search

Use *Advanced Search* on search engines.

Use more than one search engine—not all overlap.

Be specific and use Boolean logic

- **alternative energy** = **51,600,000**
- **"alternative energy"** = **9,940,000**
- **"alternative energy"** AND **wind** NOT **solar** = **639,000**

Prepared for Arizona Center for Innovation 2011, P23

Advanced Search = More Pertinent Results

wind "alternative energy " - solar

About 1,780,000 results (0.23 seconds)

Solar Wind Energy
www.siemens.com/answers   More research into green technology than any other company. Siemer

Alternative Energy - Wind, Solar, Hydro and other alt energy ...
Alternative Energy Institute, Inc. is helping public awareness of the coming energy crunch
while working on creative solutions to ease the inevitable ...
www.altenergy.org/ - Cached - Similar

Alternative Energy News
Alternative energy news and information resources about renewable energy ... **Solar Wind**
Power As the world discovers new ways to meet its growing energy ...
www.alternative-energy-news.info/ - Cached - Similar

Solar Wind Power: Generating Power In The Future
As the world discovers new ways to meet its growing energy needs, generated ...
www.alternative-energy-news.info/solar-wind-power/ - Cached

Show more results from alternative-energy-news.info

Home Power Magazine: **Solar** | **Wind** | Water | Design | Build
Independently published since 1987, Home Power magazine and HomePower.com are
resources dedicated to small-scale renewable energy and sustainable living ...
www.homepower.com/ - Cached - Similar

Solar Panels, Home **Solar** Power, DIY **Solar** Panels, **Solar** Power ...
Solar panel, **solar** heating & **wind** turbine power systems for ... Greenword blog all things on
alternative energy living, **solar** panels for homes ...
www.altestore.com/store/ - Cached

ALTERNATIVE ENERGY BLOG - **Solar**-Energy-**Wind**-Power.com

Prepared for Arizona Center for Innovation 2011, P24

TIP: Google Alerts

- Google Alerts
- Find a successful Google search
- Save as an "Alert"
- Will be pushed to your email when result of that search appears in top 10 or 20 results
- Set up Alerts for:
  - Competitors
  - Industry
  - Key customers/clients
  - YOU!

www.google.com/alerts

TIP: Website Archive Wayback Machine

The "Wayback Machine"

Provides archives of websites (some sites, some months!)

www.archive.org (in top middle of the page)

Or new beta version: http://wayback.archive.org/web/

Example: SBA (Small Business Administration) website in 2011 versus 2006.

Useful for:

Reviewing product line growth, executive changes, changes in marketing strategy, corporate branding.

SBA Website—Current 2011

Prepared for Arizona Center for Innovation 2011, P27

Wayback Machine

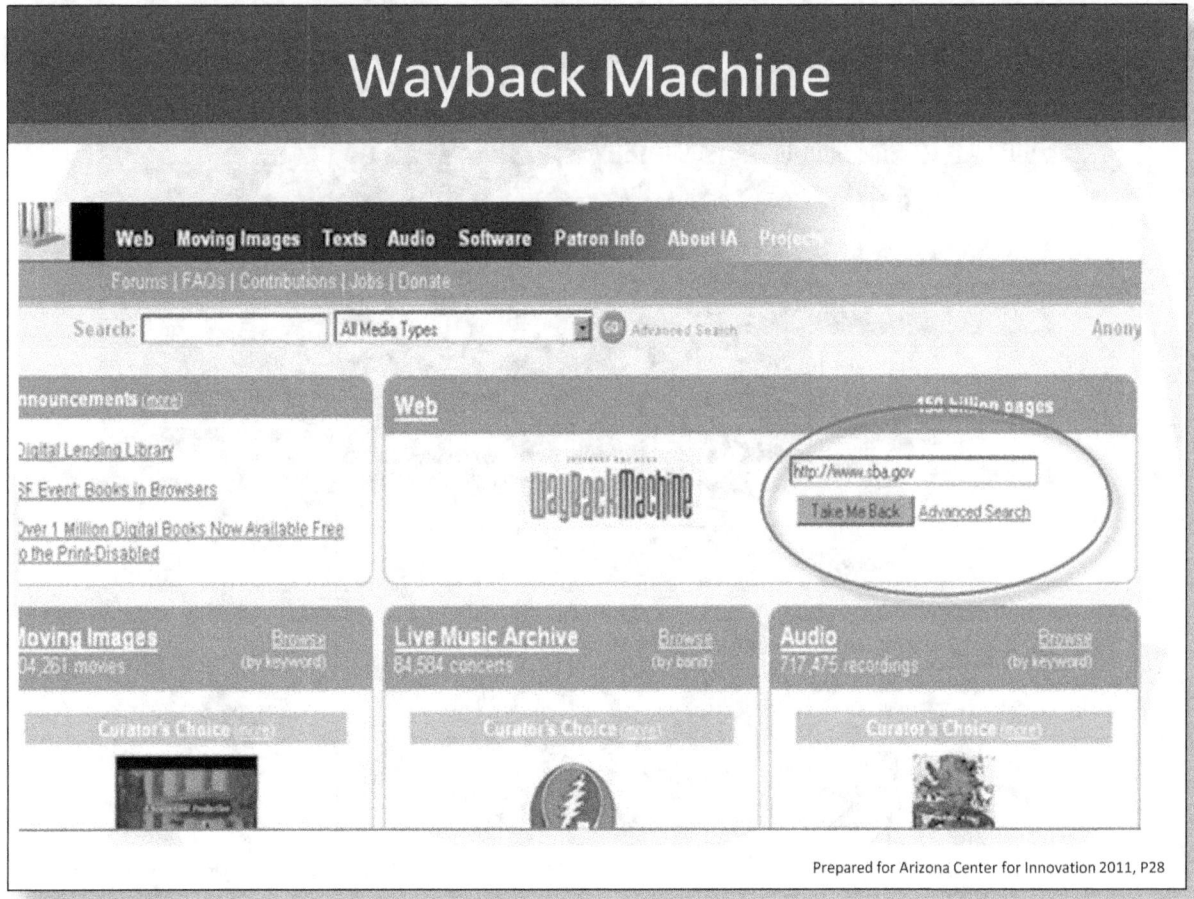

Prepared for Arizona Center for Innovation 2011, P28

Wayback Machine Results Page

...llection, with some exceptions See FAQ.

Archived Results from Jan 01, 1996 - latest

2000	2001	2002	2003	2004	2005	2006	2007	2008
19 pages	78 pages	94 pages	36 pages	204 pages	409 pages	229 pages	143 pages	102 pages
Feb 29, 2000 *	Jan 08, 2001 *	Jan 24, 2002 *	Jan 27, 2003 *	Jan 13, 2004 *	Jan 01, 2005	Jan 01, 2006	Jan 02, 2007 *	Jan 02, 2008
Mar 02, 2000 *	Jan 18, 2001 *	May 26, 2002 *	Feb 05, 2003 *	Jan 18, 2004 *	Jan 02, 2005	Jan 02, 2006	Jan 07, 2007	Jan 09, 2008 *
Mar 03, 2000 *	Feb 02, 2001 *	May 31, 2002	Feb 10, 2003 *	Feb 01, 2004 *	Jan 03, 2005	Jan 03, 2006	Jan 09, 2007	Jan 09, 2008 *
May 10, 2000 *	Feb 26, 2001 *	Jun 06, 2002	Mar 21, 2003 *	Feb 13, 2004 *	Jan 04, 2005	Jan 04, 2006 *	Jan 12, 2007 *	Jan 10, 2008 *
May 11, 2000 *	Mar 01, 2001 *	Aug 02, 2002 *	Mar 22, 2003	Feb 16, 2004	Jan 05, 2005 *	Jan 04, 2006 *	Jan 17, 2007 *	Jan 17, 2008 *
May 20, 2000 *	Mar 02, 2001	Aug 04, 2002	Mar 24, 2003	Feb 21, 2004	Jan 06, 2005	Jan 05, 2006 *	Jan 22, 2007 *	Jan 24, 2008 *
May 27, 2000 *	Mar 31, 2001 *	Aug 05, 2002	Apr 12, 2003 *	Mar 02, 2004 *	Jan 07, 2005	Jan 06, 2006 *	Jan 27, 2007 *	Jan 30, 2008 *
Jun 20, 2000 *	Apr 01, 2001	Aug 06, 2002 *	Apr 23, 2003 *	Mar 06, 2004 *	Jan 08, 2005 *	Jan 09, 2006	Jan 27, 2007 *	Jan 31, 2008
Jun 22, 2000 *	Apr 29, 2001 *	Aug 08, 2002	Apr 25, 2003	Mar 13, 2004 *	Jan 09, 2005	Jan 10, 2006 *	Jan 31, 2007	Feb 03, 2008 *
Aug 15, 2000 *	May 12, 2001 *	Aug 09, 2002	Apr 25, 2003	Mar 20, 2004 *	Jan 10, 2005	Jan 10, 2006 *	Feb 01, 2007	Feb 06, 2008 *
Oct 10, 2000 *	May 14, 2001	Aug 10, 2002	Apr 26, 2003	Mar 29, 2004 *	Jan 11, 2005	Jan 11, 2006 *	Feb 02, 2007 *	Feb 08, 2008
Oct 17, 2000 *	May 17, 2001	Aug 14, 2002 *	May 27, 2003 *	Apr 01, 2004 *	Jan 12, 2005	Jan 11, 2006 *	Feb 06, 2007 *	Feb 09, 2008 *
Oct 18, 2000	May 19, 2001	Aug 15, 2002 *	Jun 01, 2003 *	Apr 10, 2004 *	Jan 13, 2005 *	Jan 11, 2006 *	Feb 09, 2007	Feb 11, 2008
Oct 19, 2000	May 25, 2001 *	Aug 17, 2002	Jun 03, 2003 *	Apr 28, 2004 *	Jan 14, 2005	Jan 11, 2006 *	Feb 13, 2007 *	Feb 11, 2008 *
Nov 19, 2000 *	Jun 17, 2001 *	Aug 18, 2002	Jun 11, 2003 *	Jun 02, 2004 *	Jan 15, 2005 *	Jan 12, 2006 *	Feb 17, 2007	Feb 13, 2008
Dec 05, 2000 *	Jun 19, 2001	Aug 19, 2002	Jun 13, 2003 *	Jun 04, 2004	Jan 16, 2005	Jan 13, 2006	Feb 25, 2007	Feb 18, 2008 *
Dec 14, 2000 *	Jun 22, 2001 *	Aug 21, 2002 *	Jun 24, 2003 *	Jun 06, 2004	Jan 17, 2005	Jan 13, 2006 *	Feb 28, 2007 *	Feb 20, 2008 *

Prepared for Arizona Center for Innovation 2011, P29

SBA Website—2006

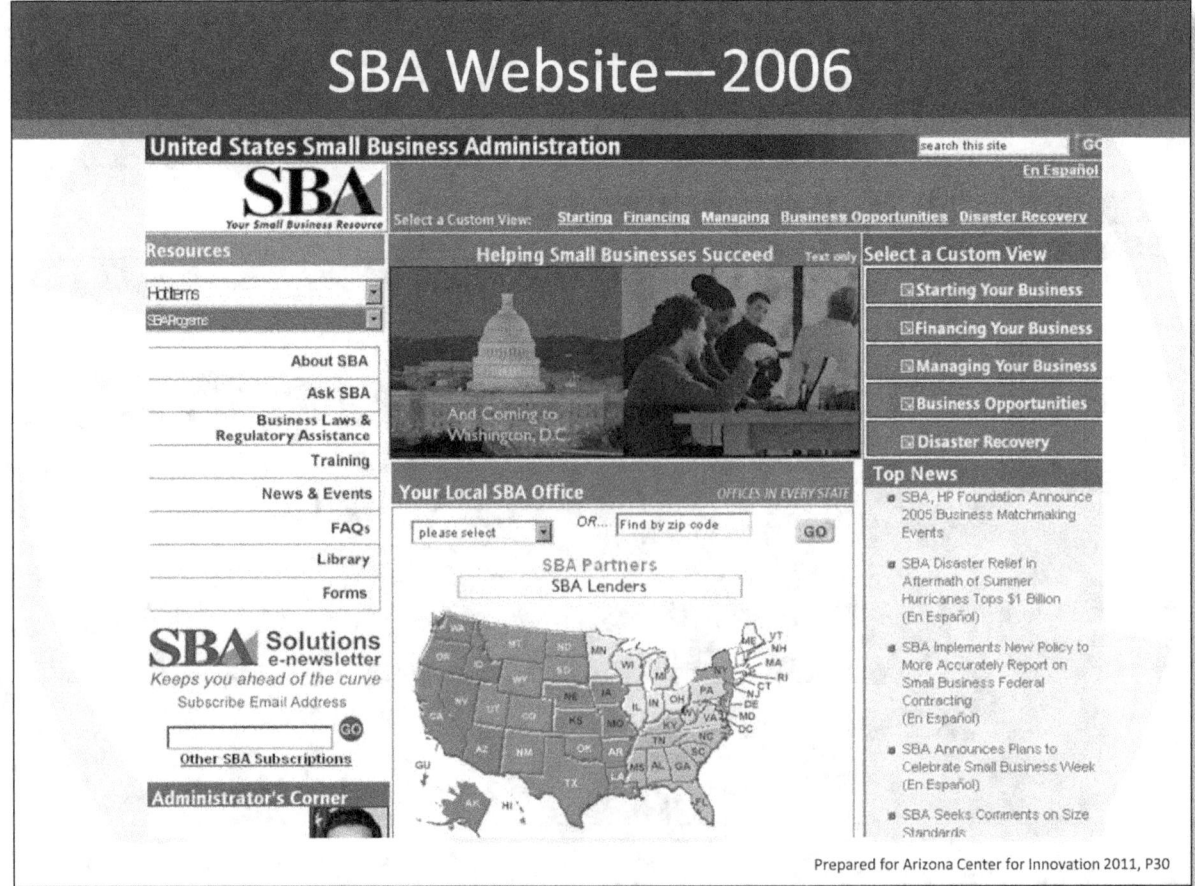

Prepared for Arizona Center for Innovation 2011, P30

TIP: Reverse Link Look Up

Reverse Link Look Up

Find out who is linking to a website

Type the website address into a search engine—preceded by the word link:

Example:

link: http://azinnovation.com/

Useful for:

Identifying partnerships, memberships, buyers' guides, clients, etc.

Prepared for Arizona Center for Innovation 2011, P31

TIP: Reverse Link Look Up

Example:

link:http://azinnovation.com/

Funding Your Innovation Through the SBIR/STTR Program - Workshop ...
uanews.org/node/40581 - Cached
Aug 5, 2011 – Contact Info & **Links**. Anita Bell Office of University Research Parks ... 520-382
-3260 rsvp@azinnovation.com **http://azinnovation.com**/node/379 ...

Funding Your Innovation Through the SBIR/STTR Program - Workshop ...
uanews.org/node/40580 - Cached
Jul 29, 2011 – Contact Info & **Links**. Anita Bell Office of University ...

➕ Show more results from uanews.org

[PDF] Business Services Available
www.ci.sahuarita.az.us/phocadownload/economic.../biz-services.pdf
File Format: **PDF**/Adobe Acrobat - Quick View
Link: http://www.aaed.com/. Google Maps: Search results for "Arizona Association of
Economic Development". Arizona Minority Business Enterprise Center ...

EquiSight student project! by EquiSight - GoFundMe
www.gofundme.com/horseracing-seniorproject - Cached
Apr 9, 2011 – Read the following Press Release for more information! **http://www.**equisight. ...
Just copy and paste our **link** onto yours or someone elses Facebook page! ... Center for
Innovation (AzCI) in May 2011 (www.**azinnovation.com**) ...

Related **Links** - Innovative Green Solu
azinnovativegreensolutions.com/related-links.htm - Cached
and add this **link** to your Related **Links** Page: <a href="**http://www.azinnovative**
greensolutions.com">Innovative Green Solutions | Your Premier Energy Audit ...

SBIR Calendar
www.zyn.com/sbir/cal/ - Cached
Underlined Conference Titles are direct **links** to their website. Updated 08/08/11 ... Contact:
Info - rsvp@**azinnovation.com**, 520-382-3260 ... Interested participants can register at
http://sbtdc.uark.edu/. Register by August 9, ...

Prepared for Arizona Center for Innovation 2011, P32

Research Matters!

Research matters because you need to know ...
- WHO your market really is.
- HOW big your potential market is.
- HOW to reach customers.
- DOES your product/service solve a problem they have?
- WHO your competitors are, what they offer, and to whom.
- WHAT are the differentiators of your competitors?
- WHAT is your own differentiation?
- Investors expect you to know.
- Sometimes you're confirming what you know already!

Prepared for Arizona Center for Innovation 2011, P33

Assignment

- What gaps do you have that research can help with?
- Who might have studied and researched pertinent information?
- Where might it have been published?
- Find trade associations and conferences that are pertinent to your product, your market, your competitors.
- Do you know who your **market** is and how to reach/find them?
- Identify your **competition** and determine what their differentiation is.
- Identify your own differentiation.
- What are the trends in your **industry**? What are growth areas? Market drivers? Who are the key players?

Prepared for Arizona Center for Innovation 2011, P34

Sales and Marketing

Building a strong marketing plan and great customer relationships

Your marketing plan helps you present your product and reach prospective customers. But what happens when you do reach them? Do you have a ready prototype; can you take payment; what does your sales channel look like? This presentation provides advice and suggestions on how to build your marketing plan and reach your first sale.

The lead contributor is Steven Wood. He is a successful entrepreneur with the background of leading several large technology and engineering companies to great successes, so he brings a variety of experience and perspective to the team. Mr. Wood is a valued Mentor for the Arizona Center for Innovation, and he sits on the advisory board for many of the incubator clients.

Building a Successful Marketing and Sales Strategy

Presented by Steven Wood

Arizona Center for Innovation
Office of University Research Parks

About the Presenter

Steven Wood

Steven received his electrical engineering degree from Northeastern University in Boston. Through his co-op period with the Massachusetts Institute of Technology, Steven worked as a systems engineer for RCA Aerospace Systems in Burlington, MA, Somerville, NJ, and Mountaintop, PA. Steven later received his degree in business administration and his master's. Entering the workforce, he partnered with the founders of Powercube Corporation, a Billerica, MA, electronics integrator. With Steven as vice president of operations, the company grew very quickly and was later acquired by Unitrode Corporation, a Lexington, MA-based semiconductor company. Leading in revenues and profits for Unitrode, Steven was promoted to vice president and general manager. He later acquired several other companies under the Unitrode umbrella. Steven, along with three others, then founded Power Convertibles Corporation, a Tucson-based power electronics company. Tripling the revenue base in two years, the business rapidly grew its base of worldwide customers. Steven along with other executives from Burr Brown sold the business to C&D Technologies, a Blue Bell, PA-based diversified electronics company where its product base remains today.

Workshop Objectives

- Marketing versus sales

- Building a sound strategy to reach and capture your customers

- Getting to that first sale

Marketing vs. Sales

- The difference between marketing and sales is far from semantics

    - Sales focuses on the needs of the seller
    - Marketing focuses on the needs of the buyer

    - Selling is preoccupied with the seller's need to convert products into cash
    - Marketing is preoccupied with the idea of satisfying the needs of the customer via the product as well as all of the other activities associated with creating, delivering, and finally consuming it

Marketing

- Everything you do to present your product or service to potential customers
  - How do I "present?"
  - What is my "product or service?"
  - Who are my "potential customers?"

- Potential customers will be attracted to your product or service if:
  - The product or service removes "pain"
  - Is clearly distinct and uniquely fit for a given task
  - Is significantly different in price to the user
  - Provides access to goods or services previously unfounded
  - Combinations of the above

Understand the Market

- How big is the total market: The size of the pie
  - How many adults are between the ages of 7 and 80?

- What portion should you focus on : The size of my slice
  - My business can appeal to and service those between the ages of 7 and 30

- What geographic area can you service well : How much pie you will actually consume
  - My business will service the 3 bordering states of X X X

- What geographic area should you focus on : How much of the slice should I actually eat
  - My business will concentrate on 3 counties closest to the office.

Know Your Competition

- Believe in the fact that there is a competitor for every new and innovative product or service created
- If there isn't a direct competitor, there are likely to be indirect competitors or alternatives to your business's product or service
- Actions:
  - Keep track of your competition regularly
  - Know their strengths and weaknesses and their evolution over time
  - Allow for "course corrections" in your business as a result of certain actions taken by your competitors

© 2011 Arizona Center for Innovation 7

Value Your Customers

- Whether active or inactive, CUSTOMERS are THE most important part of your business

- At all cost get customers, expand your customer list, and respect what they do for your business and how hard you may have worked to capture them
  - DON'T LOSE THEM!

- Customers provide your business with a bottom line … They collectively contribute to your top line, and without the top line there is no bottom line

© 2011 Arizona Center for Innovation 8

Define the Business

- Define your purpose and objective
  - Much easier said than done
  - Historically many businesses have failed as a result of improperly defining their purposes

- Examples:
  - *Personal comfort* rather than *heating & cooling*
  - *Transportation* rather than *railroads*
  - *Vision* rather than *eyeglasses*
  - *Travel* rather than *airline services*

Products or Services

- Perception
  - Study and understand how users would perceive your product or service
  - Users buy a concept—solution to a problem, simpler way to accomplish a known task, less expensive alternative without sacrificing quality
  - How are similar products perceived?
    - Create a similar perception
    - Or be distinctly different, especially if perception has been a problem

Potential Customers

- Distinguish and identify end users from all others that might be included in your chosen distribution strategy

- Regardless of the intermediary that may sell or integrate your product consider the following:
  - Who are the end users? Describe as a group
  - What geographies do the end users live in?
  - How will they see or otherwise notice your product/service?
  - How will they purchase your product/service?
  - How will the transaction take place?

© 2011 Arizona Center for Innovation 11

The Marketing Plan

- The plan maps the route between you and your prospective customers
- The plan should:
  - Articulate your market—those who will actually use your product or service
  - Identify competitors and a strategy of how the competitive threat will be resolved
  - Detail pricing, distribution, and product positioning
  - Throughout the plan show that you know your market well
- Major headings:
  - Company Objective
  - Market Analysis
  - Target Audience
  - Competitive Analysis
  - Action Plan

> TIP: BE SPECIFIC! This should be a clear game plan for your team, but also should demonstrate your knowledge and credibility to potential investors.

© 2011 Arizona Center for Innovation 12

The Trial

- Try your product or service from beginning to completion
- Look for the details - misapplied or missing altogether
- Get some sense of the customer experience

- Reality Check
  - Use friends and family as a subjective focus group
  - Get inputs - look for areas of weakness or areas to improve
  - Seek the path to perfection
  - Adjust and prepare your product or service for real focus groups

> TIP: Don't obsess or perfectionize! The reality check is just that, and you have to get out there and get started. If you are working with an advisor or incubator team, ask them for help in organizing and facilitating your group discussions.

Early Work in the Market

- At the concept stage, clearly understand what your product or service will do and what it won't do
- The plan should contain the following major headings:
  - Company Objective
  - Market Analysis
  - Target Audience
  - Competitive Analysis
  - Action Plan

Using Marketing to Sell

Properly applied marketing effort should have defined the following:

Demand as a result of market definition

Cost

Competitors

Terms & Conditions including Warranty

Execution Options

Packaging

Product Planning

Product/Service Presentation

Advertising and Promotion

Intellectual Property

Communications

Expected Demand

- Market research analysis should help predict market demand
  - This analysis should lead to decisions regarding production, lead times, service levels, etc.
- Don't attempt market introduction without the following:
  - Prototype completion
  - Preliminary performance results of prototypes
  - Technology demonstrators
  - Samples to leave behind with a potential customer
- Be able to project availability to fulfill initial demands

Cost Considerations

- Multiple costs need to be considered
- Consider the early Ford approach to cost

  "Reduce the price, extend the operations, and improve the article." – Henry Ford

- Never consider any item "fixed cost"
- Use the appropriate price to the customer to drive the cost to the right level
- Never, never, never establish a price based on your cost
- *"What earthly use is it to know the cost if it tells you that you cannot manufacture at a price at which the article can be sold?"* – Henry Ford

Monitor Competition

- Be diligent about identifying threats to your business
  - Competitive firms
  - Competitive products
  - Alternative solutions regardless of their cost or ease of utilization
- Continue periodic reviews - "up periscope"
- Allow your business to make appropriate changes based on actions of your competitors
- Be involved in your industry
- "Read the tea leaves"
- Read trade publications and review industry advertising

Terms & Condition + Warranty

- Terms & Conditions shouldn't be construed as your "Demands"
  - Review competitive T's and C's
  - Make yours reasonable and competitive
  - Use discounts / "freebies" to provoke further business or a better relationship with your clients
- Warranty
  - Does your warranty indicate the "goodness" of the product?
    - Long warranties could imply a "less than adequate" level of built-in quality

Execution Options

- How will you actually make transactions?
- Regardless of the end-consumer there are many channels to reach them
  - Direct Sales: Brick and Mortar - Consumers pay you directly
  - Direct Sales: Web & Web Stores
  - Direct Sales: Hired Sales Force
  - Manufacturers' Representatives: Contracted PT sales force
  - Stocking Distributors: Distributors purchase from you
  - Non-Stocking Distributors: in Market fulfillment option
- Other considerations:
  - Currency
  - Application of sales taxes that may apply
  - Shipping, Duties, Cartage

Product Packaging

- Packaging can be a significant distinction in your business
- Don't underestimate the need for smart packaging:
  - Packaging sends multiple messages to your customers
- Balance the packaging with your product/service
  - Don't wrap an inexpensive product with deceptive elaborate packaging
- Take advantage of multiple packaging styles:
  - Sample packaging
  - Fulfillment packaging

Product Planning

- Products convey hardware yet product planning must include all of the intangible service offered before, during, or after the sale
- New product development process:
  - Idea Generation
  - Concept Screening
  - Business Analysis
  - Prototype Development
  - Test Marketing
  - Commercialization

Product/Service Presentation

- Does your business properly present a positive result rather than a specific product or service?
- Is the business presenting all of their solutions or just a focused subset?

- How are products and service presented to the market?
  - Advertising considerations
  - Promotional material
  - Trade press

Advertising & Promotion

- Calculating ROI on advertising & promotion is nearly impossible
- Advertising can be very costly if not done properly
- Where would your clients likely see advertising in your industry?
  - Trade journals, newspapers, magazines, television, etc.
- Advertising directly to potential customers is the most effective:
  - Trade Shows
  - Seminars
  - Trade Meetings

> TIP: One of your marketing goals should be to generate LEADS that may turn into customers, referrals, etc. Always ask your prospective customer where they heard about your company or product, and set goals for each marketing activity. Track your performance and adjust accordingly.

Intellectual Property

- Don't force your business to create IP simply to pursue patent applications
- Having IP does not mean a better business or imply anything about the financial merit of the business
- IP-less businesses have the same chance at success as companies that have a huge portfolio of patents
  - Southwest Airlines

- Trade secrets are typically left unnoticed
  - Document your trade secrets and your procedures for protecting them
- Copyright your materials
- Mark materials confidential and/or proprietary

Communication

- How will you communicate about your business?
  - Financial updates to investors and stakeholders
  - Product announcements
  - Advertising
  - Seminar leadership
  - Trade press interviews
- Establish a pattern for the frequency of your communications
- Be deliberate and to the point - avoid introducing anything that can be construed as vague

Prepare to Sell

- Where will you go when the selling begins?
  - Channel selection
  - The First Order

- Are the products/services readily available to sell?

- Have you "scripted" the sales process?

- Have you considered all of the potential questions that potential customers might ask?

- Is the transaction process ready and working?

Channel Selection

- There are several combinations to consider for how best to go to market
  - Consider what your competitors are doing
- The best input for this decision will come from your potential customers
  - How would they prefer to do business with you?
  - What channel would make you distinctly better and different than others in your industry?
- Don't be afraid to be first
- Consider a combination of solutions:
  - Different geographies - currencies
  - Different cultures
  - More than one solution - i.e., direct and distribution

Prepare the Channel

- Once chosen, clearly articulate the goals and expectations to channel leadership
  - If achievement is questioned consider alternative channels
- Train, Train, Train
  - Make certain that ALL channel players are trained to do the task you want them to perform
  - Assume this to be an ongoing effort as products are added and/or channel players change
- Test, Test, Test
  - Continually ask channel managers about your products probing for their knowledge of your products or services
- Communicate, Communicate, Communicate
  - Converse or visit with your channel partners often

The First Sale

- Make certain inventories of goods or services are readily available
- Lead time for a start-up business is not a positive message
- Consider the steps to execution:
  - Have terms and conditions been conveyed?
  - Does the customer know exactly what will be delivered, when, and by what method?

- As with any customer contact, don't leave without leveraging the "connection"

Execution of the First Sale

- Most are preoccupied with having hardware ready for the first order and then resort to a used plastic bag to deliver the product
  - Pay attention to the details
  - Are your shipping materials and transportation ready?
  - Does your business have a packing list prepared or other necessary shipping documents?
  - Do you have a business invoice prepared?
- Do you have a plan ready for post-sale follow-up with the customer to assess their satisfaction
  - Be sure to contact the buyer AND user if they are different

The Sales Script

- This is not a document but a plan to follow necessary steps in order to close a sale:
  - Before a close, make sure that previous contact resolved all of the necessary items to be exchanged
  - Assess the customer's willingness and readiness to use your product or service
  - Is the timing right for an order or is there some event or milestone that must occur first?
  - Don't ask for the order if the customer is not prepared to authorize it
  - When the timing is right and all of the necessary preparatory steps have been fulfilled to the customer's satisfaction, DO ask for the order
  - Once the order has been executed, ask what conditions you must meet to continue to get orders, assuming there is ongoing demand

The Questions That Killed the Deal

- When your prospective customer asks:
  - What's the duration of your warranty?
  - What are your payment terms?
  - Does the product/service ship with any kind of data or certifications?
  - Can I select the method of shipment?
  - Are any discounts available to me?
  - Do you have any reference that I can contact about your business?
  - If I want to revise my order, who should I contact?
  - The list goes on

- Don't choke on these questions - have your response committed to memory!

Have Your Transaction Process Ready

- With an order on the buyer's desk, what's next?
  - Help the buyer e-mail the order to your "order desk"
  - Tell the customer to mail it to your company
  - Tell the customer you can't accept the order until you do a credit check
  - With gratitude, accept the hard copy of the order from the buyer and assure him/her that you will take all of the necessary actions to execute all of the items
  - Tell the buyer to call the order into your distributor
  - Explain to the buyer the difficulty in meeting the requirements of the order

Manage Your Customer Contacts

- Use your contacts to your advantage
  - Before ending any conversation with a business contact ask:
    - Do you know of anyone who can help with XXXXX?
  - Also ask as a courtesy:
    - Would it be acceptable for me to contact you if I have further questions?
  - It will get significantly harder to stay in contact with your expanding contact list. Keep at it ... It's the future of your business
- Customer Contacts
  - Established customers need constant attention
  - Maintain the contact even if there is no order imminent
    - Constantly ask about how your product or service is doing
    - Comfortable customers are likely to tell you about their experiences with your competitors

Follow-up Discussion

1. **SALES is not a 4-letter word. You have a great solution your prospective customer needs. This is a win-win solution, so be excited!**

2. One of your goals is to build and KEEP a **great relationship** with your customers. Your marketing plan helps you present your product and reach those prospective customers.

3. **Monitor your industry closely.** Look for changes in customer buying behavior; partnerships and new entrants; your competition. Stay flexible and be prepared to adjust when necessary.

4. **Know your sales channel.** This may be simple (direct sale) or complex (multi-tier channel with many partners). Understanding each participant in the channel is CRITICAL to building a successful plan.

Follow-up Discussion

5. Build a **concept drawing or prototype** of your product and use that to help you pitch your company and ideas. If you don't have capital, get creative. Use a presentation tool to simulate a software product; pull off-shelf technologies to demonstrate an application; contact your local college or university to find students, labs, prototype work; find a rapid prototype service provider; ask your incubator for ideas.

6. Be prepared when your **customer says YES**. Do you have the right manufacturing and packaging solutions? How will you deliver product? Collect payment?

Follow-up Discussion

7. Create a **tactical marketing plan** but be prepared and willing to change it. Ask your customers where they heard about you and why they decided to buy your product … and use that feedback to adjust your plan accordingly. This will likely be one of the biggest moving parts of your overall business strategy.

> TIP: Pull these discussion points together, and schedule a session with your advisors, mentors, or incubator team to brainstorm. If you have a copy of the workbook, refer to the FIRST Steps section for tips on translating your marketing strategy into an action plan and budget.

Creating the Dream Team

Surrounding your venture with the best talent: staff, mentors, advisors, and directors

Entrepreneurs often wear hundreds of different hats in the early days! It's critical to find the right support at the right time and for the right incentive. This chapter presents the 30,000-foot view of team development for early-stage ventures: founder roles; effective team building; consideration for compensation and ownership; formation of an Advisory Committee; and the formation and oversight of a Board of Directors. A case study is included on equity distribution and ownership.

The lead contributor is Corey Smith, President and CEO of bioVidria. Mr. Smith has successfully influenced the growth and success of many technology companies, and his entrepreneurial track record includes: President/CEO of ten companies; Director of sixteen additional companies; and experience raising Angel, VC, Mezzanine, and IPO financing. Mr. Smith is a Board Member for the Arizona Center for Innovation.

Creating the Dream Team

Presented by Corey Smith, President and CEO, bioVidria

Arizona Center for Innovation

Office of University Research Parks

Workshop Objectives

- Founder's Role
- Building the team
- Compensation and ownership
- Building an Advisor team
- The Board of Directors
- Final thoughts

© 2011 Arizona Center for Innovation 2

About the Presenter

Corey Smith, President and CEO, bioVidria

- Extensive experience in managing high-tech companies over the past 30 years:
  - President/CEO of 10 companies
  - Director of 16 additional companies
  - 12 years of marketing/sales at Hewlett-Packard
- Raised multiple rounds of Angel, VC, Mezzanine and IPO financings
- Managed/developed 20 "future CEOs"

The Myth: Perception Versus Reality

The Role of the Founder/CEO

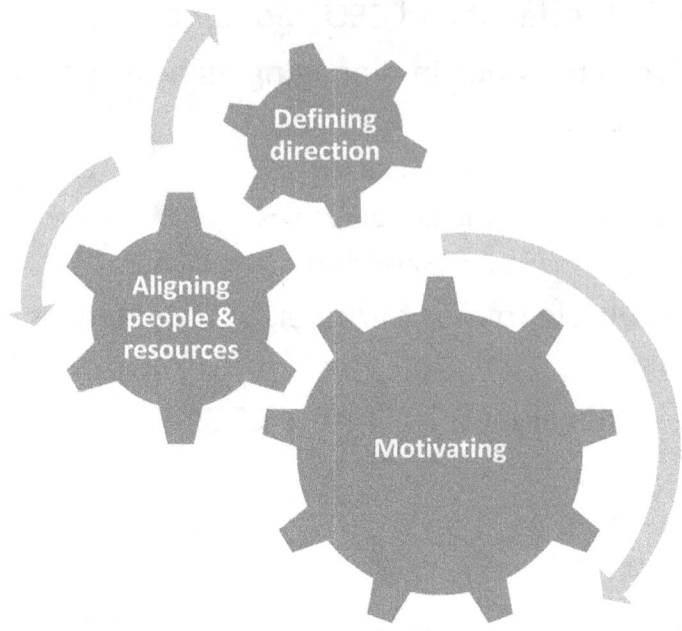

Defining Direction

- What will your company be when it grows up?
  - Market(s) served, product offerings
  - Growth strategy, 3-year planning horizon
  - Linkage of strategic and tactical plans/events
  - Partners and competitors
  - Revenues, employees, facilities, international expansion
  - Investors, valuation, exit strategy (whose "hood ornament" could you be?)
- Ability to articulate the above "matter-of-factly"
- Make it visual and real (touch it and feel it ...)
- Talk about it ALL THE TIME

Aligning People and Resources

- Building your team
- Defining responsibilities
- Funding your operation

Aligning: Building Your Team

- Who does what to whom and when
  - Job responsibilities and performance metrics
  - Org chart evolution
- Hiring (and firing)
  - Single most important thing you'll do after defining strategy
  - You're building a team ...
  - Attributes I value
    - Passionate
    - Aptitude over experience (high clock speed) and ability to grow and adapt
    - Team player and ability to subordinate
  - Don't let a bad hire linger
- Managing
  - Annual, quarterly objectives
  - Defining key breakthrough objectives
  - Linking job responsibilities with objectives FOR ALL POSITIONS

Motivating

- Teaching
- Correcting/reinforcing
- Adapting
- Growing

> *Couple of things to remember:*
>
> Establishing a company culture begins day 1
>
> The concept of "Shadow of the Leader"
>
> Catch people "Doing Things Right"

Right Team, Right Focus, Right Time

The Innovation Continuum

DISCOVERY · RESEARCH · INTELLECTUAL PROPERTY · TECHNOLOGY DEVELOPMENT · COMMERCIAL ENTERPRISE · BUSINESS INCUBATION · PRODUCTS SERVICES · COMMERCIALIZATION · RETURN ON INVESTMENT

Research	Development	Incubation	Commercialization
Focus on R&D	Assess viability, opportunity	Commercial prep Entity formation	In the market
Team: possibly early customers, other researchers	+ founders + business interests	+ management team + advisors + other partners	+ CEO + other new hires + revised advisors + board + other partners

Salary & Compensation

- Don't expect much of a paycheck from a start-up
- Long-term growth and value creation is the reward of initial sacrifice - equity over cash compensation
- New hires who can't buy in to 2 years below market pay probably aren't a good fit
- Investors do expect you to cover reasonable living expenses, but lower founder salaries demonstrate commitment to the long-term goal, and provide better profit opportunity
- Focus on healthy cash flow

© 2011 Arizona Center for Innovation 11

Compensation Considerations

- Base salary, deferred (or combination)
- Equity
- Performance-based bonus or commission
- Other soft benefits
  - Title, awards, travel, equipment, etc.
- Prepare a 3-year hiring plan by functional area (departments) and tie to option pool distribution

> Tip: Be cautious with titles, option grants, and base salary - you can always increase, but the consequences of scaling back are painful

© 2011 Arizona Center for Innovation 12

Sample Org Chart

```
┌─────────────────────────┐
│  Shareholders / Owners  │
└─────────────────────────┘

┌─────────────────────────┐
│    Board of Directors   │
└─────────────────────────┘

┌─────────────────────────┐
│        CEO or           │
│       President         │
└─────────────────────────┘

┌──────────────┐ ┌──────────────┐ ┌──────────────┐
│      VP      │ │      VP      │ │      VP      │
│ Market / Sales│ │   Product    │ │  Operations  │
└──────────────┘ └──────────────┘ └──────────────┘
```

ESOP: Not a Fable

- Employee Stock Option Plan (ESOP)
  - Provides employees with company ownership through purchase of shares at discount from preferred offering
  - Key component of an overall compensation package
  - Employees have vested interest in company's success
- Average for technology startups:
  - 15–20% for recruiting C-Team, future employees, partners
  - Average technology founder retains < 4% of company going public

> Tip: don't get sidetracked by percentage ownership; 51% of nothing is nothing. Focus instead on maximizing company value!

3-Year Option Pool Breakdown Example

Level	#	Option %	Extended	Options per Individual	Theoretical Value Yr 3
CEO/President	1	6.00%	6.00%	107,143	3,600,001
VP Level	4	1.25%	5.00%	22,321	750,000
Director/Senior	12	0.30%	3.60%	5,357	180,000
Contributor	30	0.10%	3.00%	1,786	60,000
Admin/support	20	0.02%	0.40%	357	12,000
Advisor/Board	5	0.40%	2.00%	7,143	240,000
			20.00%		

Option pool size	357,143	(20% pre Angel & VC investment)
Total shares outstanding	3,571,429	
Company value year 3	120,000,000	(8X multiple on revenue of $15M)

The Equity Pie Fable

■ Founder

<u>Research stage</u>:
Valuation is speculative
Technology still in assessment
Founders have 100% ... of what?

The Equity Pie Fable

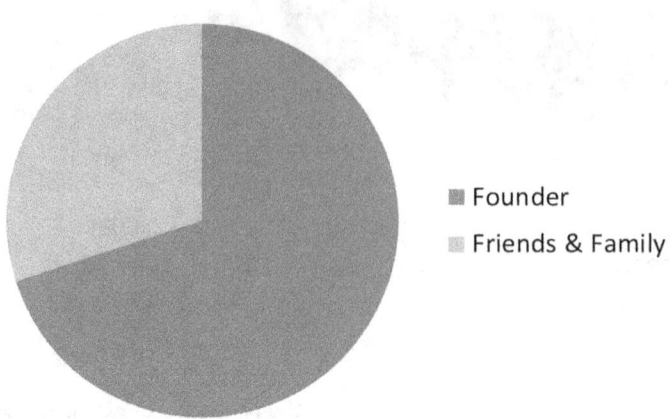

■ Founder
▨ Friends & Family

<u>Raise Friends & Family money</u>:
Founder resources tapped out
$$$ needed for prototype development
Common stock issued
Founders @ 70%

The Equity Pie Fable

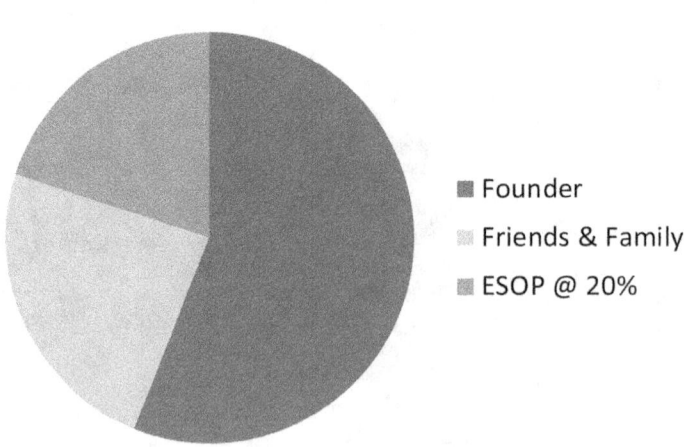

■ Founder
▨ Friends & Family
▨ ESOP @ 20%

<u>ESOP established</u>:
20% shares reserved
Initial customer engagements
Founders keep 56%

The Equity Pie Fable

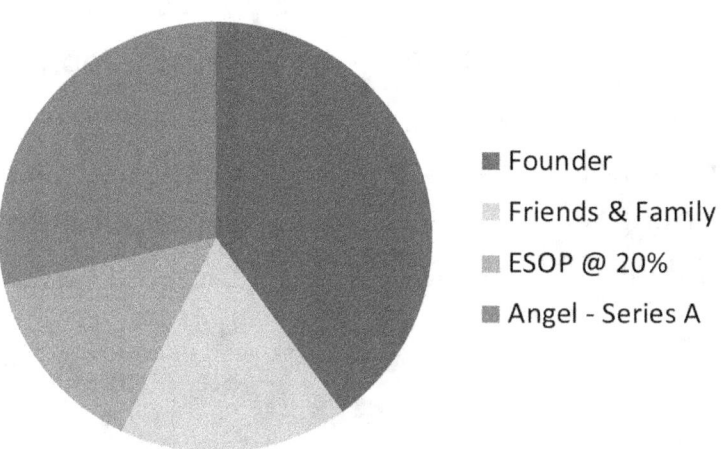

- ■ Founder
- ▦ Friends & Family
- ▨ ESOP @ 20%
- ■ Angel - Series A

Angel Investment:
Preferred shares issued
Money used to complete product, launch sales
Founders now at 40%

Post-VC Round: Founder @ 28%

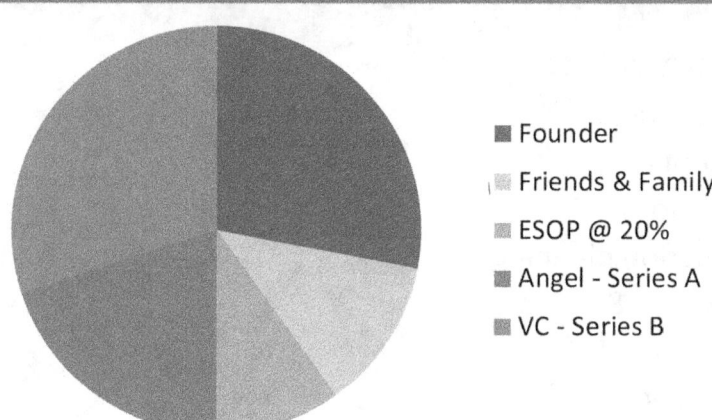

- ■ Founder
- ▦ Friends & Family
- ▨ ESOP @ 20%
- ■ Angel - Series A
- ▨ VC - Series B

	Shares	Investment	Valuation	Post VC
Founder	1,000,000	50,000	NA	28%
Friends & Family	428,571	150,000	500,000	12%
ESOP @ 20%	357,143			10%
Angel - Series A	714,286	500,000	1,750,000	20%
VC - Series B	1,071,429	1,500,000	5,000,000	30%
Total	3,571,429			100%

Role of Advisors versus Board of Directors

- **Advisors**
  - Advice and perspective
  - Skill augmentation
  - Management experience
  - Confidant
  - Guide
  - Domain expertise
  - Contacts

- **Board of Directors**
  - Legal responsibility
  - Binding action
  - Fiduciary role to shareholders
  - Dictated by company bylaws
  - Strategically inclined

Putting Advisors to Work

- **Help most with:**
  - Introductions
  - Concepts
  - Technology
  - Production planning
  - Marketing & Sales
  - Finance & HR
  - Operations

- **Help least with:**
  - Day-to-day operations

Advisors

- Where to find:
  - Friends and family
  - Instructors
  - School referrals
  - Attorneys or CPAs
  - Your first and only advisor (hint: get your first and you are on your way!)
- How to compensate:
  - Philanthropic: thrill of doing it again
  - Potential of future involvement or association
  - Options (develop a long-term plan)
  - Cash (be very careful)

Board of Directors

- Will be mandated upon taking in outside money
- Equity as compensation
- Role is big picture, financial oversight, C-level hiring
- Be proactive in advance of raise to shape creation
  - 5-person board (you, investor, +3)
  - Long-term commitment: 3+ years
  - Seek directors who will commit sufficient time to have general understanding of your business, market, etc.
- One director likely to roll off as second raise completed
- D&O insurance
- Quarterly meetings at the outset
- Advisory Board and Board of Directors can coexist

Management Section of Business Plan

Don't forget to include:

- <u>Organizational structure</u>: key management roles and people (exiting/planned) along with career highlights, duties, resumes

- <u>Management compensation</u> and ownership: agreements, bonus, benefits, ESOPs, etc.

- <u>Advisory and Board of Directors</u>: list and include 1–2 line bios plus any other supporting services or affiliations; include targeted Board of Director members

- <u>Other shareholders, rights and restrictions</u>: investment terms; capitalization table; notable investors

A Few Final Thoughts …

- Don't fall victim to the "Superman syndrome" - the effectiveness of a leader is measured by the output of his/her team
- A simple strategy will always prevail over a complex one: $.8^5$ is a small number (32.8%)
- Good market characteristics will often reward even mediocre execution - pick it carefully
- External constituents don't live in your day-to-day world - you can never overcommunicate
- An investor's motivation is simple - when do I get my 10X cash back?

Summary

- Founder's role
- Building the team
- Compensation and ownership
- Building an Advisor team
- The Board of Directors

Follow-up: If you haven't yet done so, conduct a SWOT analysis of your team strengths and weaknesses. Put together a short list of the kind of talent and support your venture needs, and add that to your elevator pitch!

Building Your Financials

Understanding the function of financial statements in your daily operations, and in forecasting future successes

Effective financial statements are the foundation for any successful business. They can be used as a means to track and measure progress, as compass to set your directional course for future growth, as a storyboard for capital investment, or as a tool to communicate and report company success to your stakeholders. Yet they also represent a significant challenge for many new entrepreneurs. This presentation provides a close look at financial statements, introduces forecasting methods and strategies, and provides general advice on how to get started.

This chapter is presented BeachFleischman PC, a premier public accounting firm based in Tucson, Arizona, and serving clients worldwide. BeachFleischman PC is a key partner to the Arizona Center for Innovation and provides exceptional support for the incubator clients.

Basic Financial Statement Preparation and Forecasting

Presented by:
BeachFleischman PC

About the Presenters

520-321-4600

George E. Henderson, CPA

George Henderson is an accounting and assurance shareholder with BeachFleischman PC. He has planned and performed audits, reviews, and compilations of numerous privately held companies. George is director of our employee benefit plan practice group and our science and manufacturing practice segment. He coordinates income tax planning and compliance services and performs other business consulting. George has over 20 years of audit experience in public practice.
ghenderson@beachfleischman.com

Eric B. Maneval, CPA

Eric Maneval is an accounting and assurance senior manager at BeachFleischman PC. He has planned and managed numerous audits and reviews of health care, not-for-profit, manufacturing, and high-tech start-up organizations. He is the head of our emerging issues committee and specializes in complex equity transactions. Eric has over 7 years of audit experience in public practice. emaneval@beachfleischman.com

BFC●
BEACHFLEISCHMAN

Workshop Objectives

This workshop will provide the following:

- An introduction to, and the use of, basic financial statements: balance sheet, statement of income, statement of cash flows, and notes to financial statements.

- Overview of forecasting methods.

- Strategies to forecast revenue, expenses, and financing for startup ventures.

Basic Financial Statements

- Balance Sheet
- Statement of Income
- Statement of Cash Flows
- Notes to Financial Statements

Balance Sheet

- Also called the statement of financial position
- Snapshot of a business's financial condition at a specific moment in time.
- Comprises assets, liabilities, and owners' or stockholders' equity.
- At any given time, assets must equal liabilities plus owners' equity.
- The statement answers the question "What assets and liabilities do we have?"

Statement of Income

- Otherwise known as a profit and loss statement or statement of operations
- A summary of a company's profit or loss during a given period of time.
- Tracks revenues and expenses so that you can determine the operating performance of your business over a period of time.
- The statement answers the question "Did we make money?"

Statement of Cash Flows

- Reports the *cash* generated and used during the period of time covered by the financial statements.
- Reported in three segments
  - Operating activities
  - Investing activities
  - Financing activities
- Statement answers the question "How did you spend and earn your money?"

Statement of Cash Flows

Operating	Investing	Financing
• Operating income • Changes in assets and liabilities • Depreciation Amortization • Income from Investment • Gain/Loss on sale of equity securities • Gain/Loss on sale of assets	• Increase intangible assets • Purchase of fixed assets • Proceeds from disposal of fixed assets • Return on investment • Collections on notes receivable • Advances on notes receivable • Proceeds from sale of equity securities	• Net repayment on notes payable bank (line of credit) • Principal payment on long-term debt • Borrowings on long-term debt • Distributions/dividends • Proceeds from issuance of Common Stock

Footnotes and Disclosures

- Significant policies
- Company activities and relationships
- Components of inventory
- Accrued expenses and debt detail
- Related party transactions
- Commitments and Contingencies

Basis of Accounting

Accrual

- Cash basis adjusted for timing differences to match expenses and revenues
- GAAP

Cash

- Based on actual cash receipts and cash expenditures of the company
- Not GAAP

Uses of Financial Statements

- Internal reporting
- Bank
- Investors
- Potential investors
- Others

Internally vs. Externally Prepared

- Internal reporting - management prepares

- External reporting - the use of a CPA firm to increase the creditability of the financial statements
  - Audit
  - Review
  - Compilation

Forecasting

- Two available formats
  - Forecast
  - Projection

- Two basic methods
  - Presentation of expected financial position and results from operations
  - Presentation of expected cash flows

Forecasting

- Forecast
  - A prospective financial statement that presents an entity's expected financial position

- Projection
  - A prospective financial statement that presents an expected financial position under one or more hypothetical assumptions

Forecasting

- Requires significant assumptions by management

- Financial statements should be restricted as to use

- A complete set of financial statements do not have to be produced

Forecasting

- Keys to consider
  - Revenues: How much will you sell?
  - Expenses: What will it cost you to make these sales?
  - Investing: What assets will you need?
  - Financing: How will you pay for it?

Forecasting - Revenue

- Step 1: Budgeting your sales volume

  - Drives the rest of the process
  - Answers the question "How much money do you expect to generate?"
  - Asks the question "What will you need to generate that money?"
  - Important to be realistic

Forecasting - Revenue

- Step 1: Budgeting your sales volume - you should consider:

  - Existing sales volume
  - Demand for your product
  - Market penetration & saturation
  - Reasonable growth
  - Sustainable growth

Forecasting - Expenses

- Step 2: Budgeting your costs

  - Answers the questions
    - "What do I need to create enough product to meet my sales volume goal?"
    - "How much will it cost to generate those sales?"
    - Important to consider all costs

Forecasting - Expenses

- Step 2: Budgeting your costs - you should consider:

  - Facilities
  - Furniture
  - Machinery and equipment
  - Distribution locations/methods
  - Workforce size
  - Materials needed

Forecasting - Expenses

- Step 2: Budgeting your costs - you should consider:

    - Insurance
    - Repairs
    - Utilities
    - Marketing and advertising
    - Travel
    - Office supplies
    - Other

Forecasting - Expenses

- Step 2: Budgeting your costs

- Fixed costs
    - Costs that won't increase (decrease) based on volume within a range of production
        - Building
        - Machinery
        - Equipment
        - Furniture

Forecasting - Expenses

- Step 2: Budgeting your costs

- Variable costs
  - Costs that will increase (decrease) based on volume within a range of production
    - Materials
    - Labor
    - Utilities

Forecasting - Expenses

- Example

  - ABC Company purchases a copy machine that can copy 100 pages per minute.
    - Fixed cost: the machine
    - Variable costs: each piece of paper used, ink, toner

Forecasting - Financing

- ## Step 3: Financing

  - How will you fund the cost of your business?
    - Debt financing
    - Equity financing
    - Operations

Forecasting - Financing

- ## Debt Financing
  - Operations can be funded through borrowing
  - Types of debt
    - Conventional
    - Convertible
    - Hybrid
      - Detachable warrants
      - Other sweeteners

Forecasting - Financing

- **Conventional Debt Financing**
  - Standard loan with a bank or other financial institution
    - Term loan
    - Line of credit
  - Generally requires monthly payments of principle and interest
  - Interest rates fixed or variable
    - Most banks can only offer variable rates
    - Instruments exist to fix the rates - swaps

Forecasting—Financing

- **Convertible Debt Financing**
  - Loans generally from private individuals and entities
  - Short and long term "Bridge Loans"
  - Payments
    - Can require regular principal and interest payments
    - May defer payment
  - Interest rates are generally fixed and typically higher than conventional bank loans

Forecasting - Financing

- **Convertible Debt Financing**
  - Debt is convertible into an equity interest in your company
    - Common shares
    - Preferred shares
  - Conversion feature can be triggered by either the debt holder, the company, or both

Forecasting - Financing

- **Hybrid Debt Financing - generally required by "angel financers"**
  - Conventional or convertible debt with added sweeteners
  - Warrants
    - Common shares
    - Preferred shares
  - The cost of the sweeteners can be substantial
    - The actual cost of the debt
    - Cost of complying with accounting requirements

Forecasting - Financing

- **Equity Financing**
  - Operations can be funded through investment
  - Types of equity
    - Common stock
      - Classes of stock with differing rights and features
    - Preferred stock & sweeteners
      - Redemption features
      - Conversion features
      - Classes of stock with differing rights

Forecasting - Financing

- **Operations**
  - Existing and expanded operations can generate positive cash flows
    - Excess of revenues over the costs related to obtaining those revenues
  - In general, this is a secondary source of financing in the early stages of a business until volume reaches certain levels

Forecasting

- Internal vs. External Forecast
  - Companies should consider whether to use a CPA firm to compile their forecast
    - Added credibility
    - Expertise

Workshop Summary

- Introduction to, and the use of, basic financial statements: balance sheet, statement of income, statement of cash flows, and notes to financial statements.

- Overview of forecasting methods.

- Strategies to forecast revenue, expenses, and financing for startup ventures.

Follow-up

If you haven't yet done so, put together your initial financial statements and present those to your partners and team members for discussion and feedback. Ask your incubator team and their partners for assistance. Here are a few examples of websites that provide great templates and information:

- http://www.us.smetoolkit.org
- www.sba.gov
- www.SCORE.org

Note: If you are working with the Arizona Center for Innovation, many of our partners provide these services. If you are anxious to put a draft together yourself, ask for the Financial Modeling Package, created by Michael J. Arnold. Mr. Arnold is a Mentor with AzCI, a successful entrepreneur, and is the Director of the Engineering Management Program and Professor of Practice at the University of Arizona.

Good luck!

BFC●
BEACHFLEISCHMAN
Prepared by BeachFleischman for Arizona Center for Innovation 35

Funding

10

Considerations for funding your new venture

Ventures evolve as they move through the innovation continuum from initial concept to market success. As the venture evolves, so does funding: founder cash; grants; angel investment; venture capital; debt financing; etc. Building a strategy to effectively pursue the right kind of money at the right time can make all the difference for a new venture. This presentation addresses various types of funding and uses current company examples.

The lead contributor is Marie Wesselhoft, President and Co-Founder of MSDx. Ms. Wesselhoft has a successful track record with over thirty years of experience in the healthcare industry, and held the position as the Director of the Arizona Center for Innovation for five years before stepping down in 2010. She continues to provide support and workshop training to the incubator clients, and is a Board Member for the Arizona Center for Innovation.

Funding Considerations

Presented by Marie Wesselhoft
President and Cofounder of MSDx

About the Presenter

Marie Wesselhoft, President and Cofounder, MSDx

Marie has over 30 years of business experience with a successful track record in health care. Marie held positions such as VP/general manager, VP marketing, area VP of sales, and product manager throughout her 20-year career at Cardinal/Baxter/American Hospital Supply Company. In her role as general manager of the Scientific Products, an $850 million business, her responsibilities included management of a national sales and marketing team comprised of more than 140 people. Throughout her career she has had opportunities to launch $100 million diagnostic product lines, negotiate partnership agreements, and manage key accounts, as well as facilitate the integration of teams for acquisitions and divestitures. During her years at Humana Hospital she was both a laboratory director and medical technologist. She also has experience with several health care start-up companies in her work at the Arizona Center for Innovation. She graduated from the University of Wisconsin with a BS in medical technology and completed an MBA at the University of Chicago.

Funding Varies by <u>Type</u> of Business

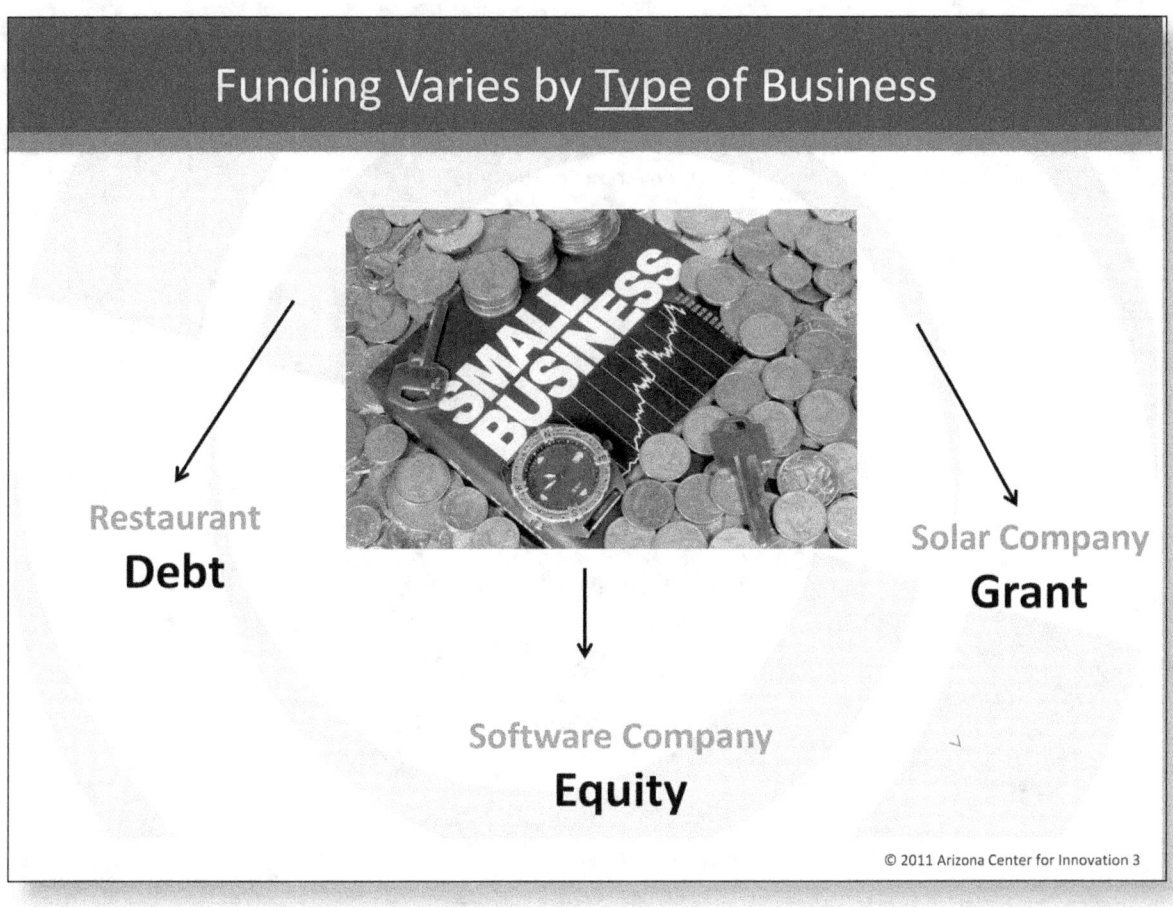

Restaurant
Debt

Software Company
Equity

Solar Company
Grant

Funding Varies by <u>Risk</u>

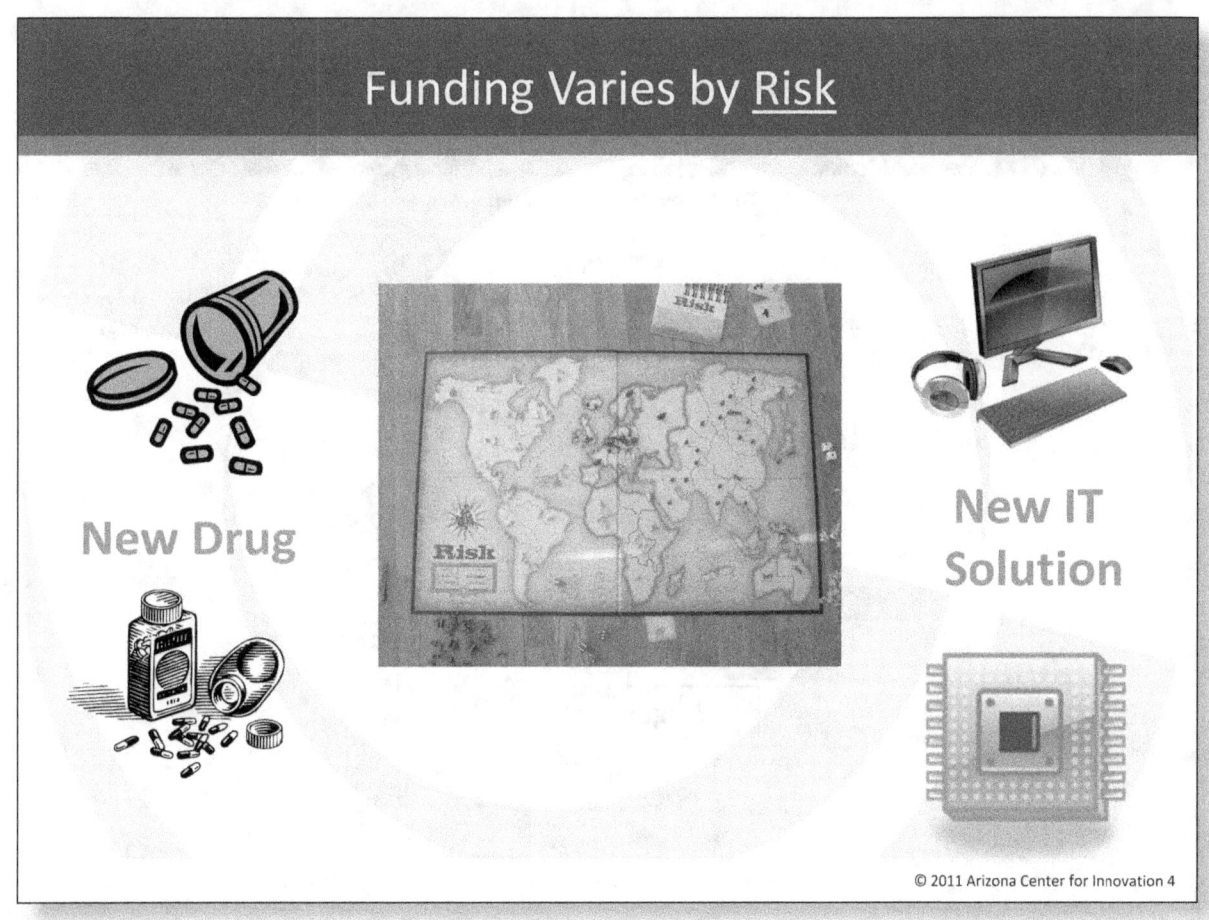

New Drug

New IT Solution

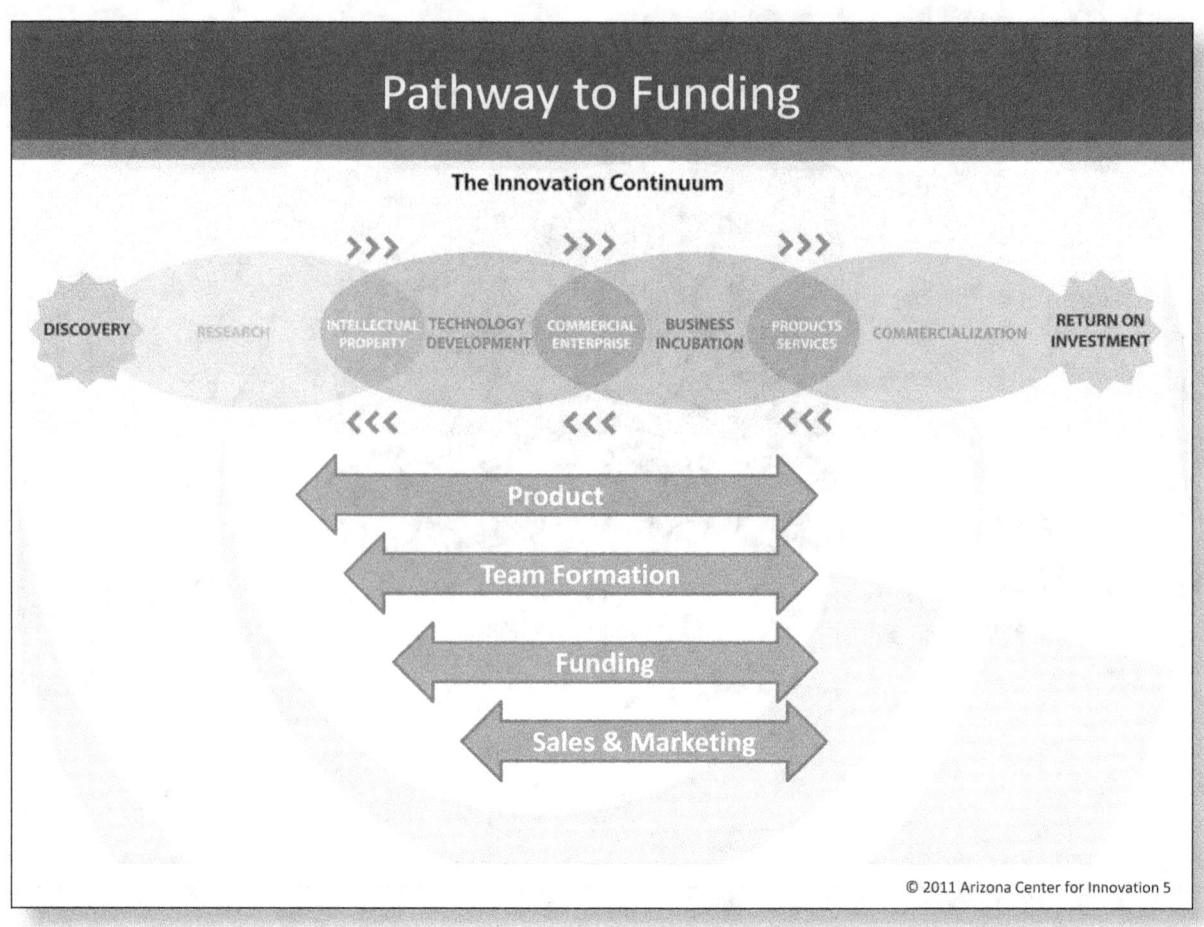

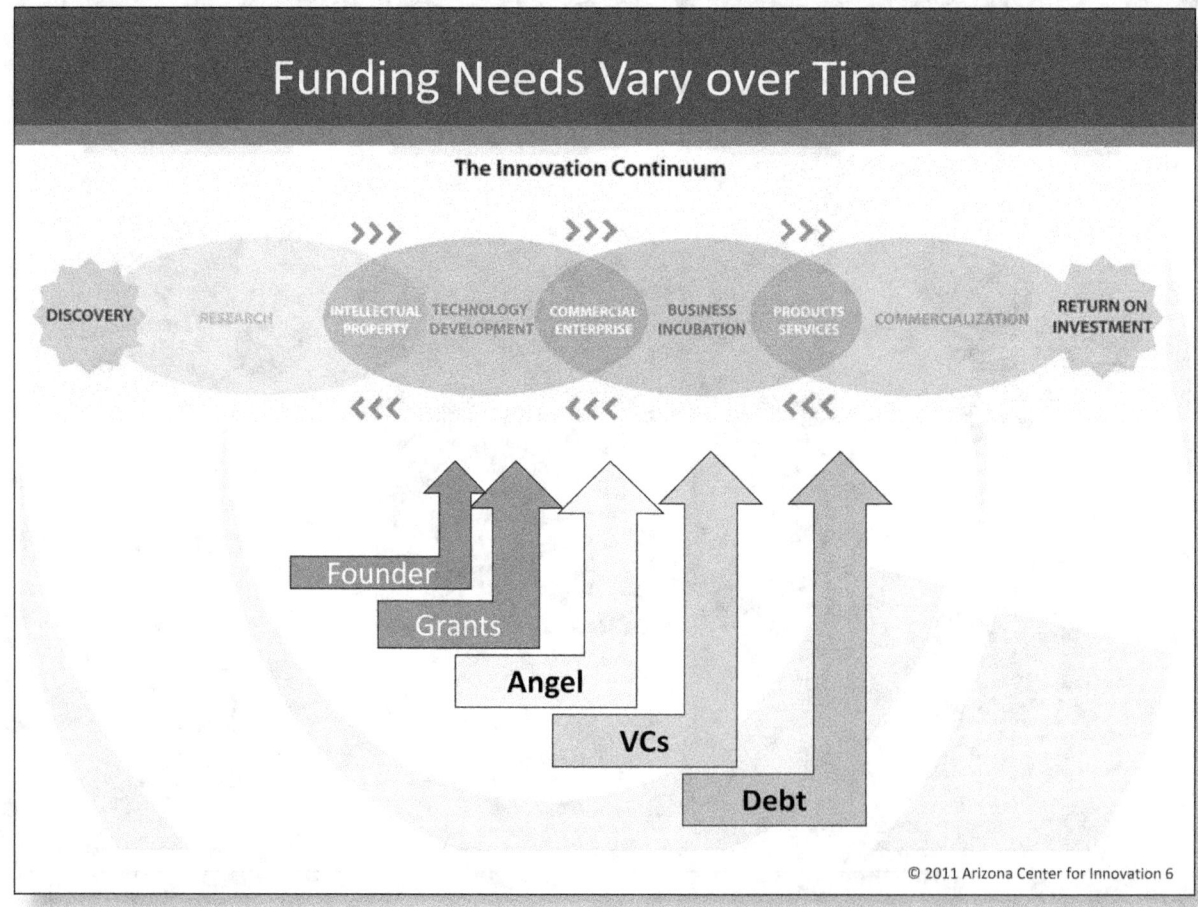

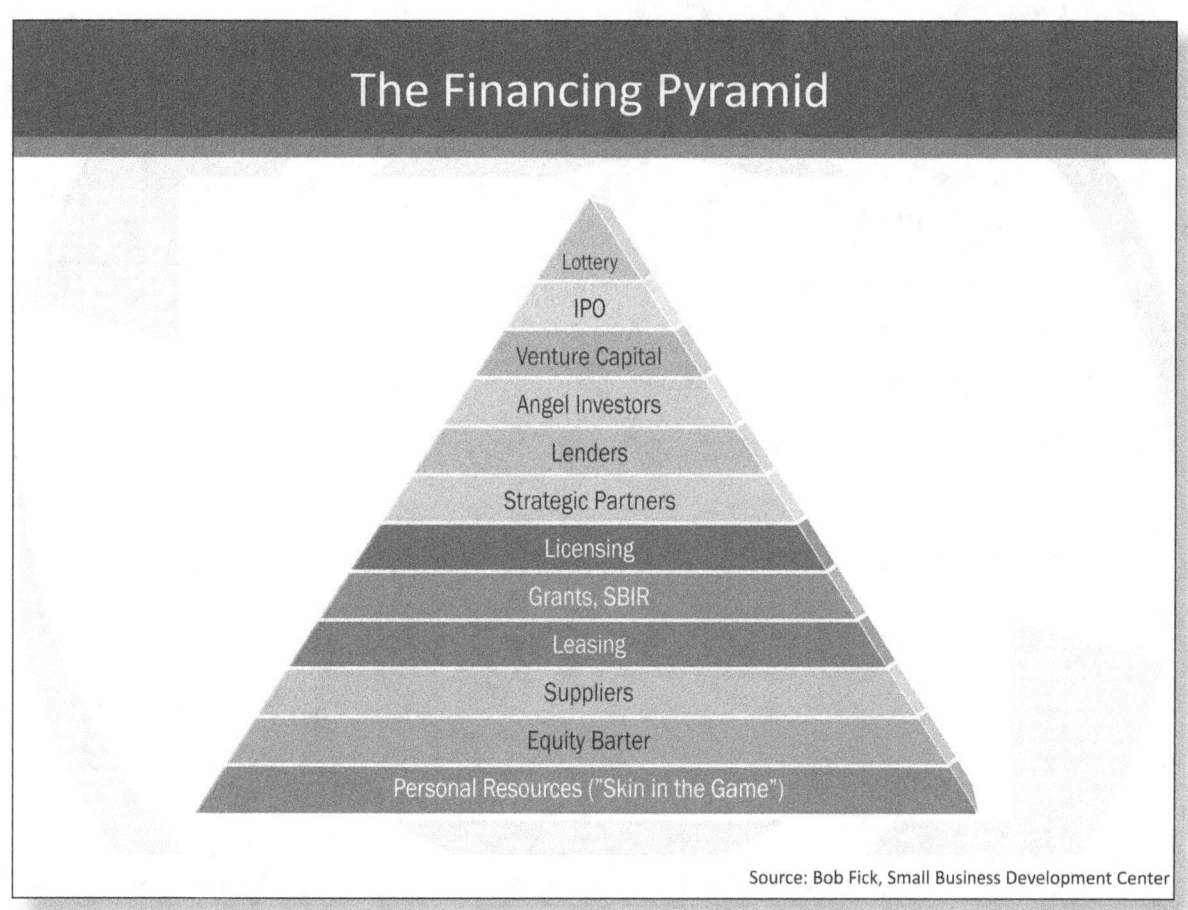

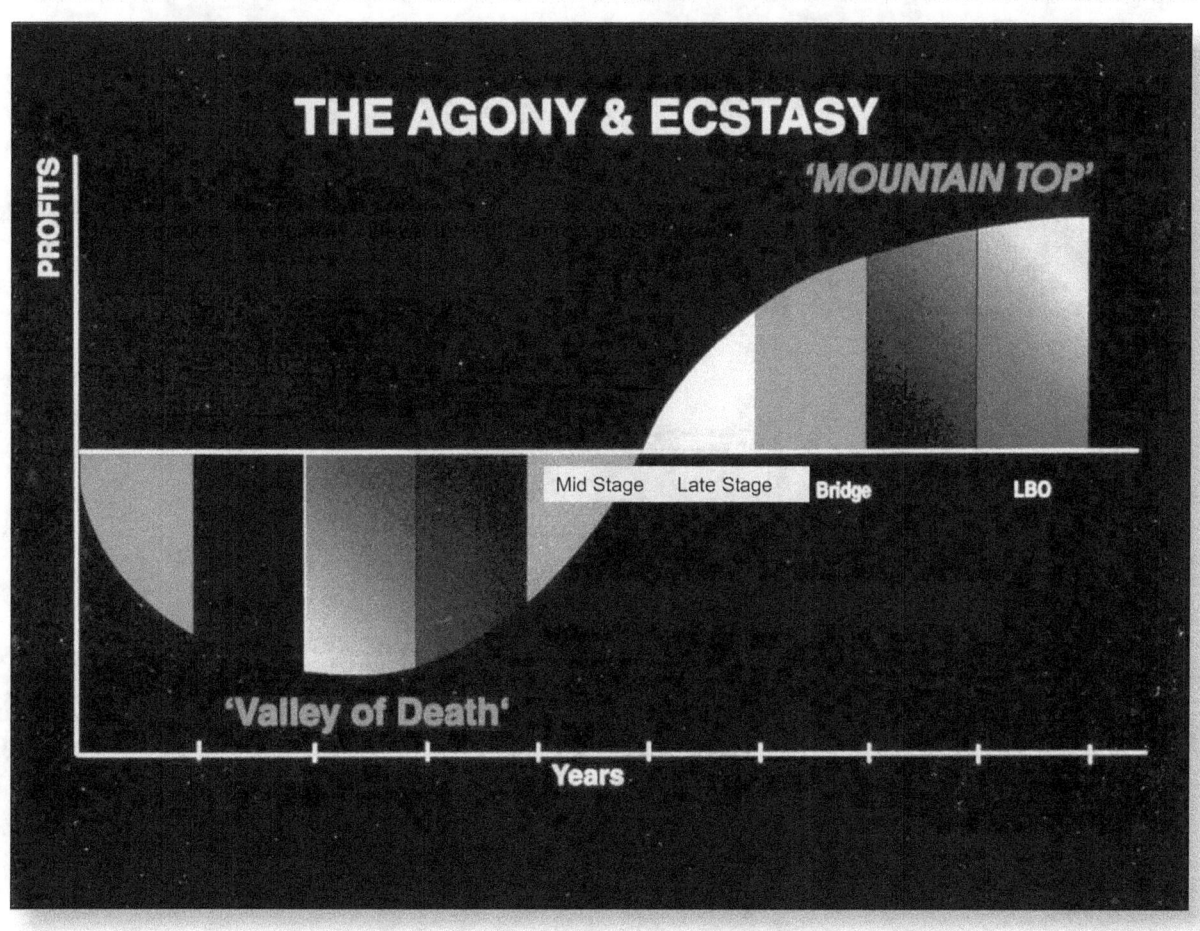

Preparing to Seek Financing

- Business plan
- Financial forecast
- Elevator speech
- Presentation
- Amount required and purpose
- Valuation
- Exit strategy

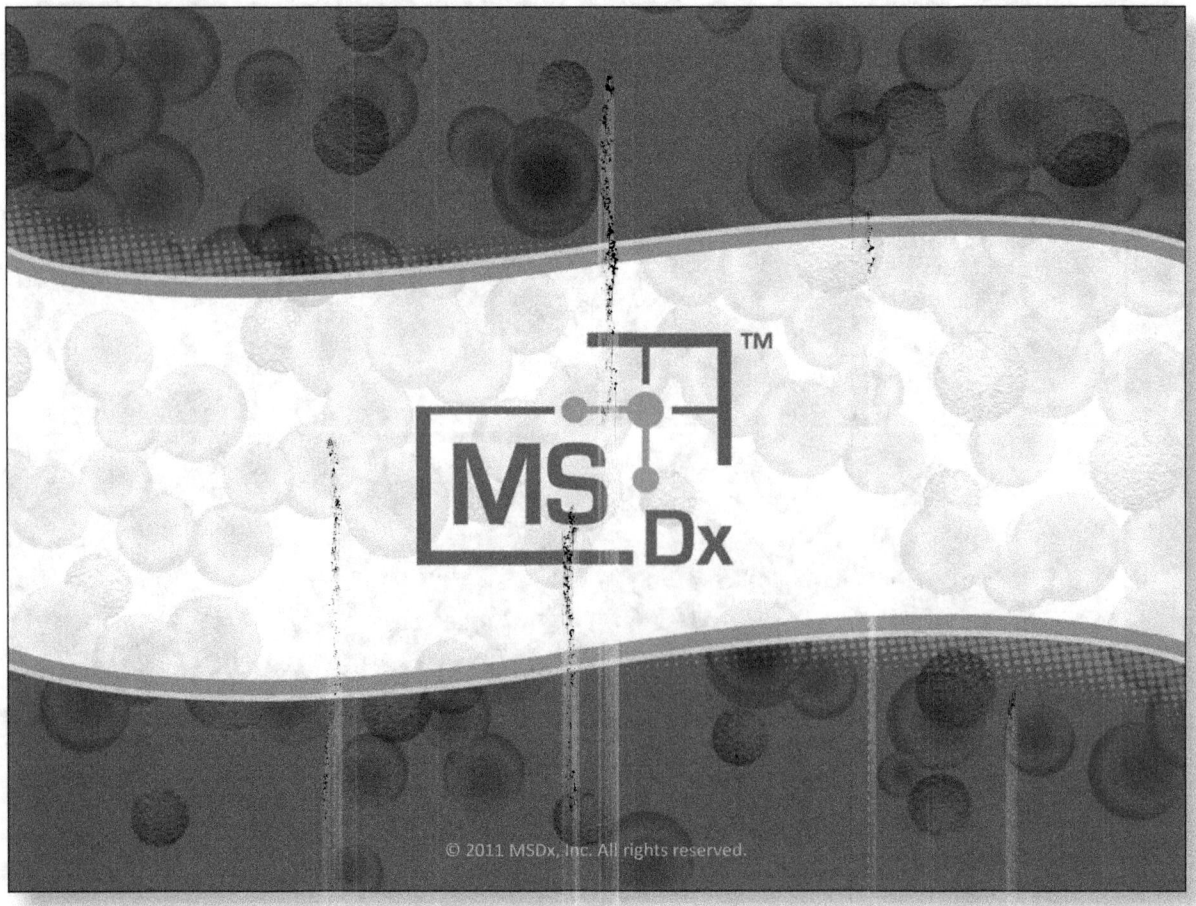

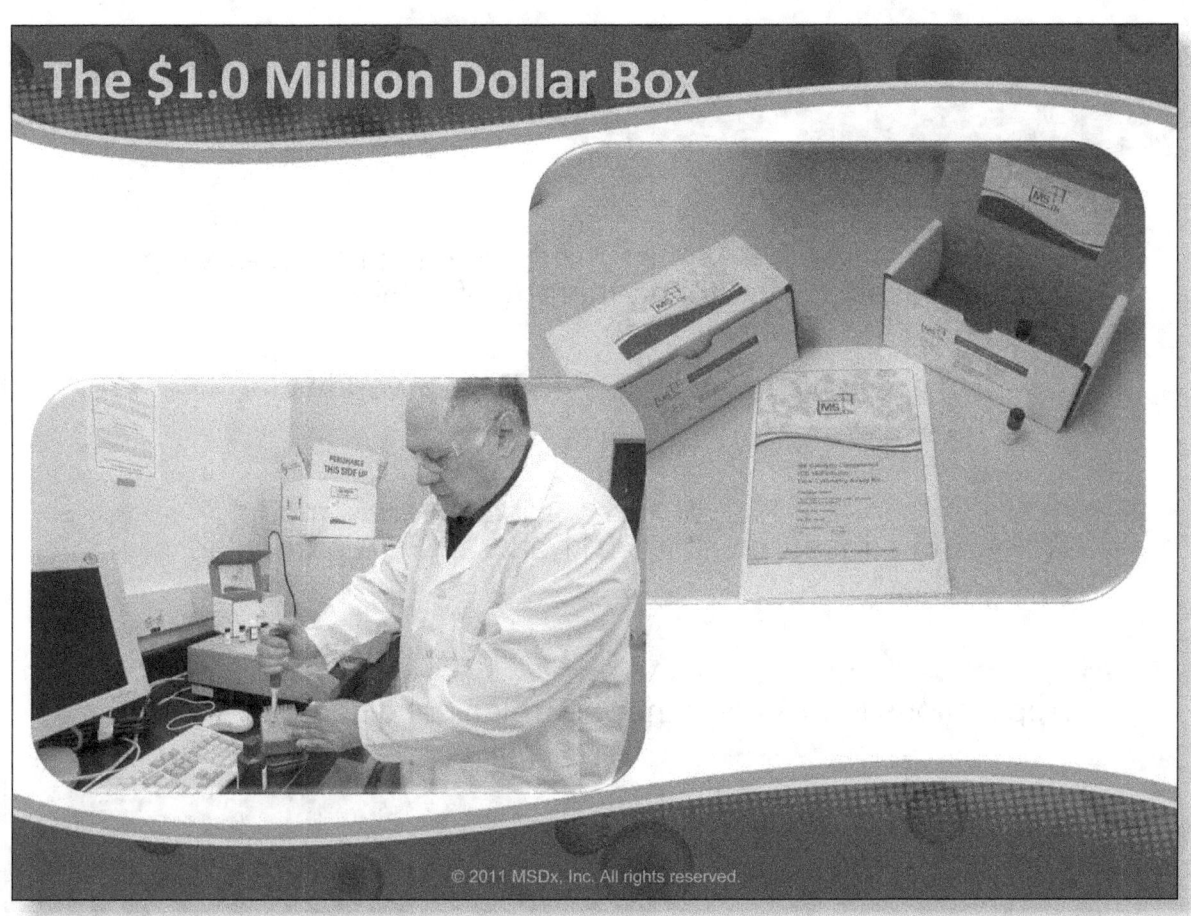

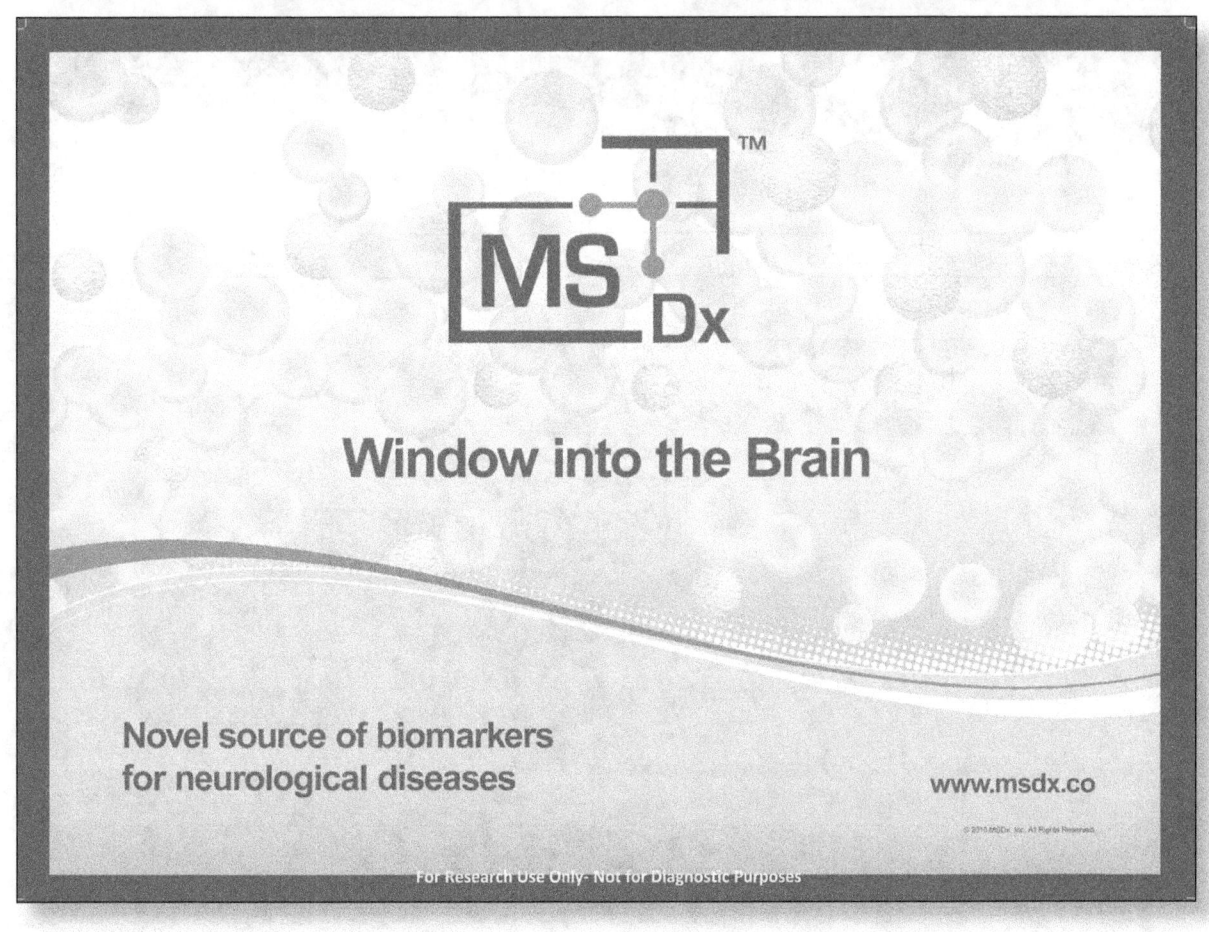

Window into the Brain

Novel source of biomarkers
for neurological diseases

www.msdx.co

The MSDx Opportunity

Personalized Medicine Solution - Panel of blood-testing products used in monitoring therapy effectiveness

Laboratory Testing Market - $46 Billion worldwide, growing at 7%

Proven Business Model - Recurring revenue model. Releasing a research kit in 2011 and an FDA product in 2013.

Innovative Technology - *Window into the Brain* - Applications in MS and other neurological diseases

MSDx Funding

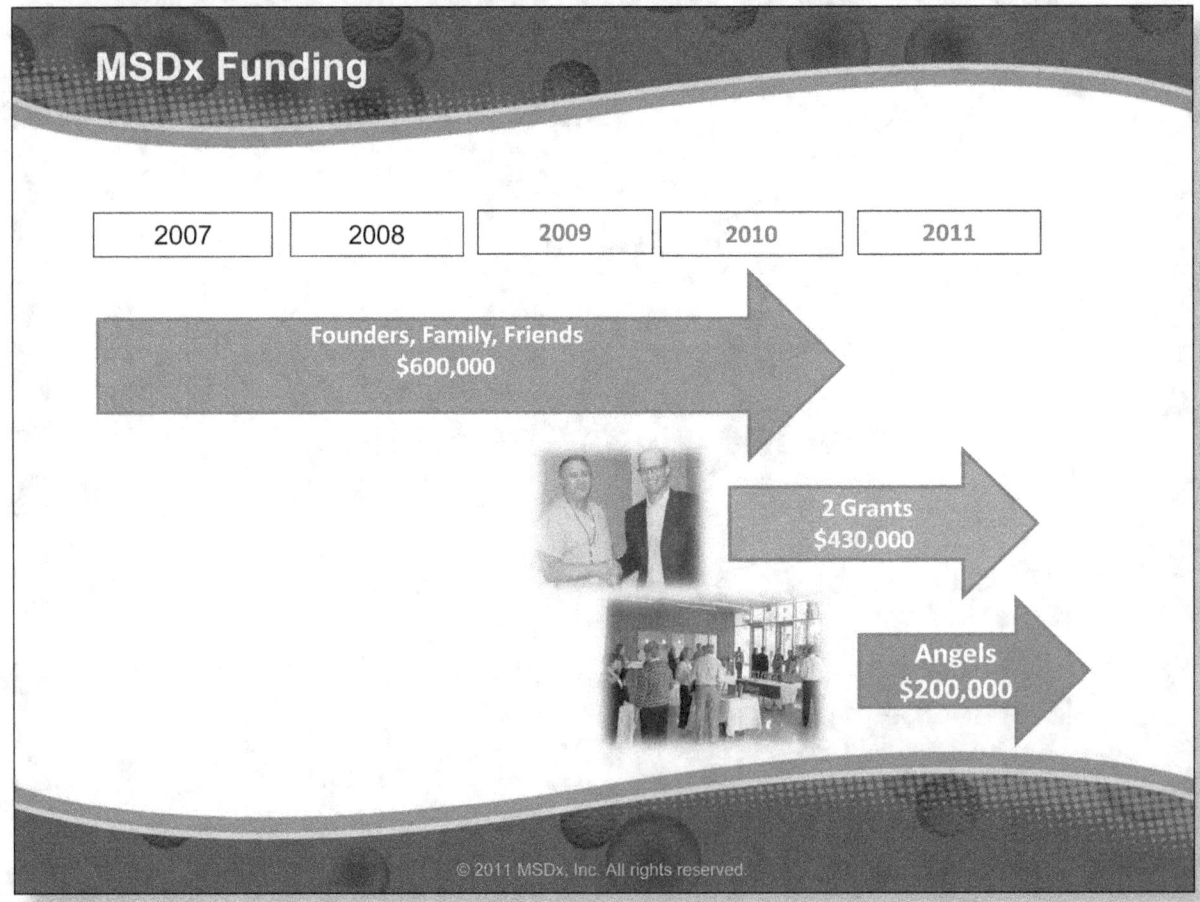

| 2007 | 2008 | 2009 | 2010 | 2011 |

Founders, Family, Friends
$600,000

2 Grants
$430,000

Angels
$200,000

Funding - Our Lessons Learned

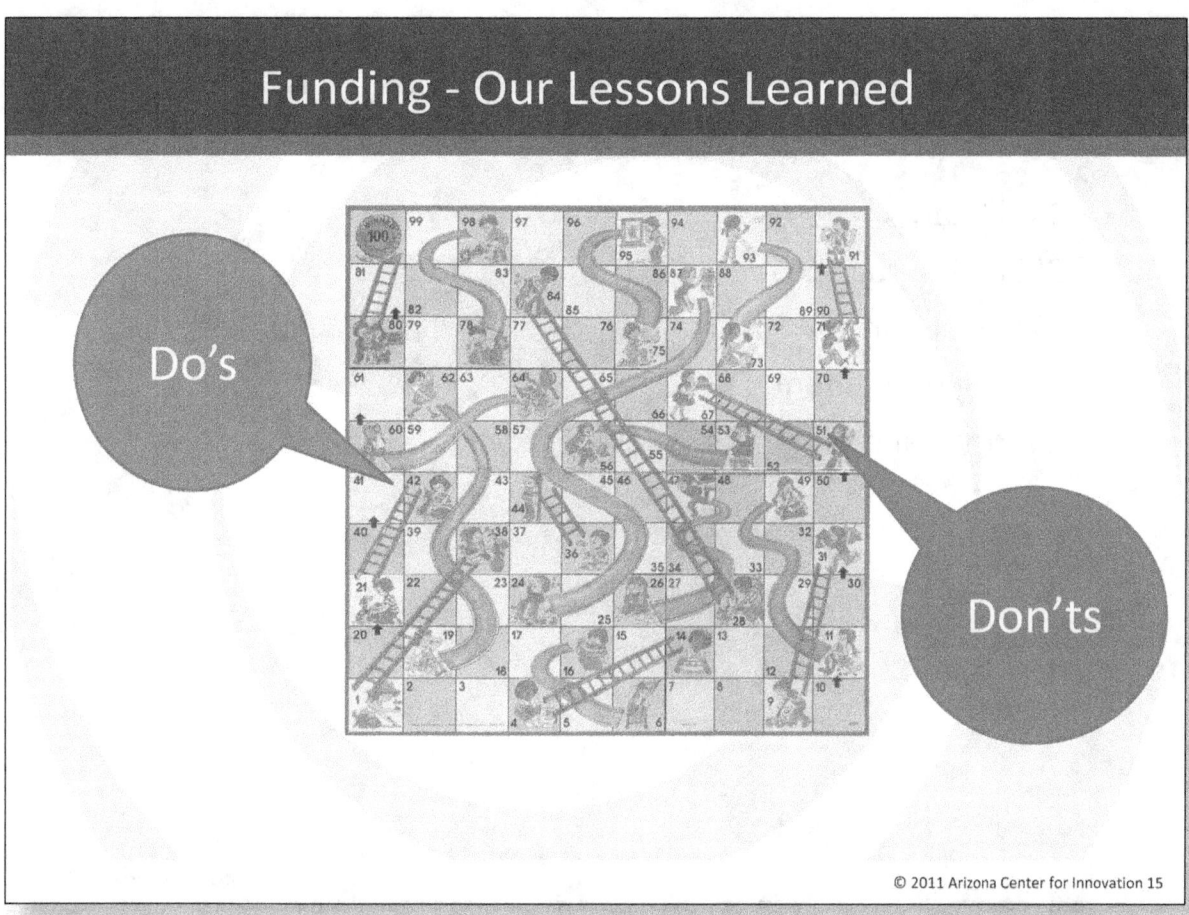

Do's

Don'ts

Founder, Family, and Friends

- No one funds your job
- Think before you leave your day job.
- Think about it long and hard!
- Credit card
- Your assets are on the line
- Establish a process to handle cash and time
- Represents ownership percentage
- Share in proceeds from company sale
- No obligation to repay?
- Very risky

Early Debt

- Credit cards
- Obligation to repay
- Interest bearing
- Leasing equipment
- Priority claim on assets vs. owners

Grants

SBIR/STTR

- Allocated from federal agency budgets
- Over $2 billion available
- Matching research
- Phases I and II; "Phase III"
- Excellent pathway to VC or partner
- Grant or contract; not debt or equity
- Little concern about IP issues
- http://www.grants.gov/

> Tip: Cast a broad net when researching grants. You may find new opportunities through your industry or affiliations, for minority-owned businesses, etc. Grants often bring added value and help validate your progress and are a critical part of your funding strategy.

MSDx Receives Two Grants

Track Record: Currently 2 of 8

$ 204,000
QTDP Grant

$226,495
AZ Innovation Grant

**MSDx Goal:
Grants for 30% of Cash**

National Institute of
Neurological Disorders and Stroke
National Institutes of Health
Reducing the burden of neurological disease...

National Science Foundation
WHERE DISCOVERIES BEGIN

Our
Do's
&
Don'ts

Fast Forward
Speeding Treatments To People With MS

Angel Investors

For consideration:
- Repay obligation
- Represents ownership percentage
- Voting/nonvoting
- Share in dividends/distributions, if any
- Claim on assets secondary to creditors
- Share in proceeds from company sale
- Often received in stages
- Individual high net worth investors
- Angel groups
- Match your market
- Exit timing and risk profile must fit

© 2011 Arizona Center for Innovation 21

Angel Investors

Who is an angel investor?
- SEC accredited investor
- >$1 million in net worth or $200K income
- Generally invest $25-250K in a deal
- Generally make several angel investments
- Roles: Lead investor, investor/advisor, passive investor

Typical angel investment:
- $250-1M in total (multiple investors)
- Valuation: $1-3M
- Angel equity: 20-40%
- Expected ROI: 60% annual or 10x

Source: Angel Capital Association

Angel Investors

Angel organization statistics:
- Number of orgs 1999 = <100, 2006 >250
- ACA memberships = 127 from 43 states
- ACA attendees 2002 = 35, 2007 = 330
- Average number of investments = 7.4
- Total $ invested per org = $1.8M
- Average $241,000 per round
- Average per angel investor = $31,000

Investment brackets:
- $0-250K: Pre-seed - P, F, F, & F
- $250-1.5M: Seed/start-up - angels
- $4-10M+: Early/later stage - VCs
- Investment gap $1.5-4M

Source: Angel Capital Association

MSDx Angel Investors ...

National and Local Angel Groups

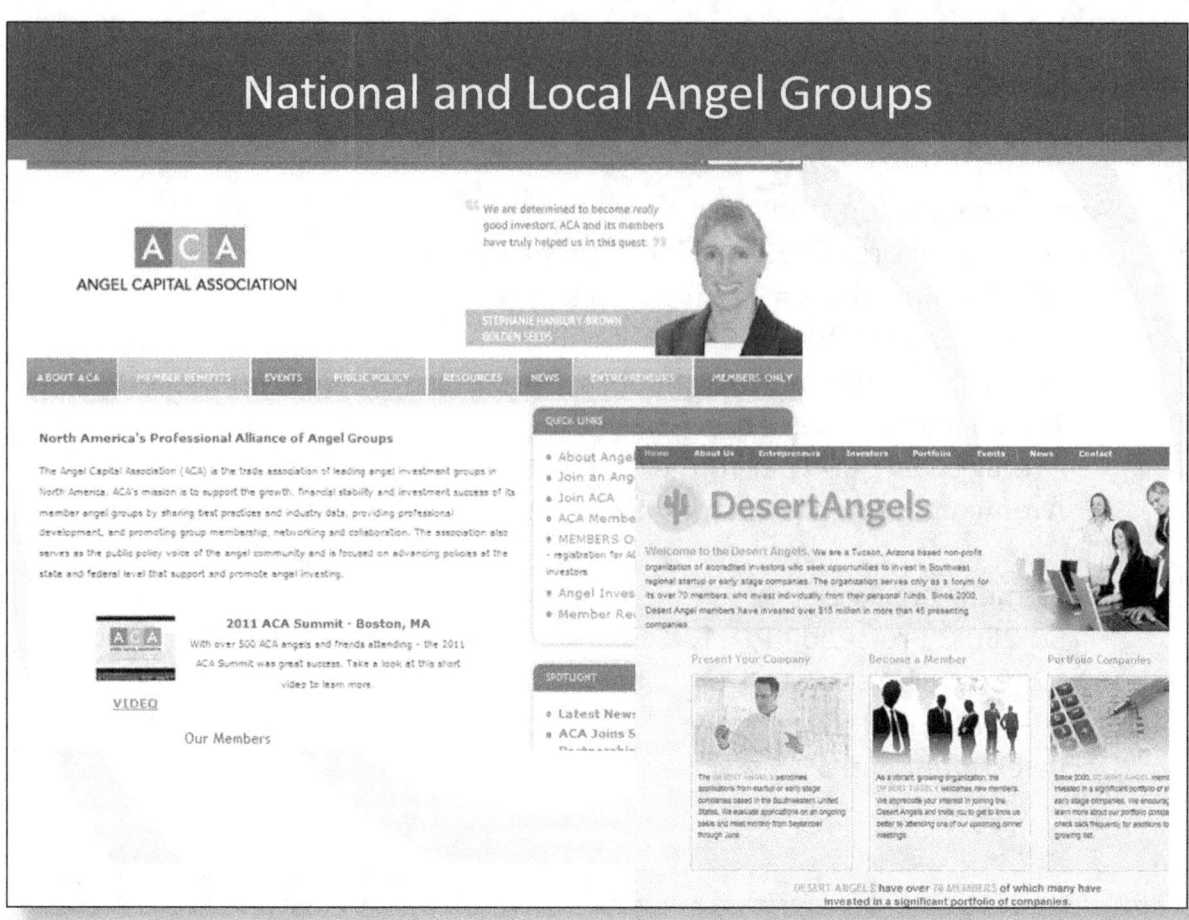

Investment Environment

- <1 in 20 start-ups obtain angel financing
- <1 in 500 start-ups are VC financed
- <1 in 5,000 new companies go public
- <1 in 25 angel deals see VC money
- <1 in 250 angel-funded companies go public

Does My Company Qualify for Angel Investment?

- Am I willing to give up some ownership and control?
- Will my company generate significant revenues and earnings in 3-7 years?
- Do I have a strong management team?
- Have I made a personal investment in the company?
- Do I have a clear picture of the market and a realistic plan for meeting my sales goals?
- Will my company produce a superior return for investors?
- Am I willing to accept board of director decisions?
- Do I have a 3-7 year exit plan?

Why Investors Turn Down Deals

- *Quality of management*
- *Size of opportunity*
- Rate of market growth
- Product quality
- Competition
- Barriers to entry
- Stage of development

Considerations

The money:
- How much is needed?
- What is the financial strategy?
- How will you structure the deal and set valuation?
- What is the exit strategy and expected ROI?
- Does the entrepreneur understand financial concepts?

Valuation:
- No formula - it is a "black art"
- Must be estimated
- Comparative, discounted cash flow
- Back into it using required ROI
- Subject to a number of factors
- Typically $1-3M ... OR LESS!

Considerations

Back into it:
- Investment: $1M
- Profit in year 5 (exit): $2M
- Industry P/E: 15x
- Valuation in year 5: $30M
- Required investor's ROI: 60% or 10x
- Required investor's valuation: $10M
- % of company required: 33%
- Today's post-money valuation: $3M

Valuation
- Management team: 0-30%
- Size of opportunity: 0-25%
- Product or service: 0-10%
- Sales channels: 0-10%
- Stage of business: 0-10%
- Size of this round: 0-5%
- Need for more financing: 0-5%

Considerations

Due diligence process:
- Don't start unless it appears there is a deal
- Business plan review (vision etc.)
- Management presentation and discussion; site visit(s)
- References
- Competitive, IP, financial analysis
- The terms sheet and deal

Typical deal terms:
- Common or preferred stock, sub debt with warrants
- 1st position for liquidation, dividends, conversion
- 1st rights for registration, participation, antidilution
- Voting, board member or observer
- Performance - milestones, tranches, ratios, executive compensation

MSDx Term Sheet Highlights

- **Pre-money value**

- **Series A2 round**

- **Warrants**

- **Liquidation preference**

- **Redemption rights**

- **Antidilution**

- **Board (5)**

Angel vs. Venture Capital

	Angel	Venture Capital
Number of investors	400,000	900
Number of deals	50,000	2,500
Total annual investment (2006)	$20 billion	$26 billion
Investment size	$.5 million	$7-8 million
Stage of investment company	Start-up	Later
Amount of capital required to prove the business model	Under $3 to $5 million	Over $3 to $5 million
Years before being able to exit	2 to 5 years	10 to 12 years
Most likely value of the company at the time of the optimum exit	Under $50 million	Over $100 million
Willingness to relinquish control of important financial decisions	Not always required	Almost always required

Source: Angel Capital Association

Venture Capital Considerations

- Specialize by industry sector, geography, and stage of development
- Primarily focus on later-stage companies
- May take 4-6 months to complete

- For the select few
- Rapid revenue growth
- Market dominance
- Barriers to entry
- Demand significant returns
- Workable investment window
- Professionals

Investment Requires Exits

- Investing only works if the investors can get their money back - even if it takes a while
- The traditional venture capital model no longer works, restricted by types of exits a VC may need
- Still quite a good time for entrepreneurs and angel investors

Interesting resources on VC reporting:

- PricewaterhouseCoopers MoneyTree™ report: www.pwcmoneytree.com/MTPublic/ns/index.jsp
- National Venture Capital Association: www.nvca.org/

Two Paths for Exit

MS Dx ™

Acquisition	**Expand to Other Neurological Diseases**

31 acquisitions in 18 Months

Deals at 3–4x revenue

Candidates: Alere, Athena

Buying sales & filling gaps

Diagnostics & pharma buyers

Alzheimer's

Parkinson's

Lessons Learned

1. You are never done
2. It is about them, not you
3. It takes 100% longer than you think
4. Investments are in companies, not products
5. Nothing is as scary as payroll without cash
6. Multiple sources
7. Always do the right thing
8. The best capital is revenue

Summary

- The innovation continuum describes the chain of processes that are involved when bringing a product from concept to market.

- As the product moves along the continuum and the new venture develops, different types of funding may be needed. Each will present unique opportunities that should be considered when creating a funding strategy.

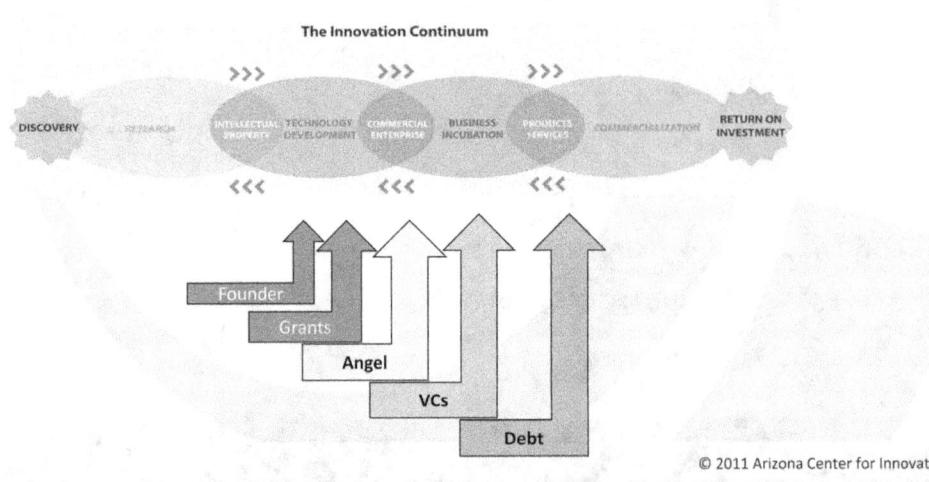

The Innovation Continuum

Great Resources

Handy online tools for exit and other considerations:
www.Early-Exits.com
www.AngelBlog.net
www.BasilPeters.com

Starting a Business

Legal considerations

Starting a business can be fun and exciting, and often legal considerations fall last on the planning list. They may be difficult to navigate or seem unnecessary to address, but one wrong mistake can stop your venture in its tracks. This presentation addresses entity formation, partnerships, capitalization, and common mistakes often made during the start-up phase. It also provides a short list of basic agreements that every new business must have.

This chapter is presented by Snell & Wilmer LLP, a full-service business law firm with more than 400 attorneys practicing in nine locations throughout the western United States and Mexico. Snell & Wilmer LLP is a valued mentor and partner with the Arizona Center for Innovation and has served many start-up ventures in our community.

Starting a Business:
Legal Considerations

Presented by Snell & Wilmer LLP

Office of University Research Parks

Snell & Wilmer LLP

Lowell Thomas, Partner, Business and Finance Group

(520) 882-1221 ~ lthomas@swlaw.com

Lowell serves as lead counsel for equity and debt financings, mergers, acquisitions, and other restructuring transactions across a broad range of industries for public and private corporations. He also advises emerging growth companies in the formation and growth stages and advises corporate boards on governance matters. Having practiced law in Canada for the first half of his career, Lowell has extensive connections in business, the capital markets, and government on both sides of the border.

Snell & Wilmer LLP

Angela Perez, Associate, Business and Finance Group, and Chair of the Bioscience Industry Group

(602) 382-6354 ~ alperez@swlaw.com

Angela's practice is concentrated in business and finance, focusing on venture capital and private equity, mergers and acquisitions, regulatory compliance, and commercial agreements. Her experience includes representation of clients in various industries, including bioscience, medical research, health care, OTC drugs and pharmaceuticals, and product manufacturing. Angela's experience also includes representation of clients at various stages of the company life cycle, from start-up to liquidation.

Learning Objectives

- Understand the advantages and disadvantages of the different types of entities available for your business and the appropriate entity or entities for you based on your business objectives.

- Understand the most common mistakes that a business owner may make in attracting personal liability with respect to the operation of his or her business.

- Understand the critical contractual agreements that a business owner should consider at the commencement of any business operations.

Agenda

1) Protecting your personal assets by forming a company
2) Selecting the right form of entity
3) How to form a company
4) Capitalizing a new company
5) What it means to have partners and how to bring them in
6) Basic agreements every new business must have

Protecting Personal Assets by Forming a Company

Who should form a company
from which to operate their business?

Every business owner
(i.e., no sole proprietorships or general partnerships)

Protecting Personal Assets by Forming a Company

Why form a company
from which to operate your business?

Protect your personal assets
from claims

Piercing the Corporate Veil

As a general matter, corporations/LLCs are treated as a separate legal person, which is solely responsible for the debts it incurs and the sole beneficiary of the credit it is owed. In order to receive the benefit of this general principle, owners must avoid certain "mistakes" that might allow a creditor to look through the corporate/LLC form and hold its shareholders, members, or directors liable for the debts of the entity.

When a creditor is permitted to hold the owners liable for the debts of the company, the creditor is deemed to have *"Pierced the Corporate Veil."*

Does a Company Guarantee Asset Protection?

Must prevent "piercing of the corporate veil"

1) Ignoring corporate formalities ("alter ego" theory)
   - Shareholder abuses the privilege of incorporating and fairness demands that the shareholder be held personally liable
   - Arizona courts may find corporation is an alter ego when shareholder:
     - Treats the assets of the corporation as his own
     - Uses corporate funds to pay private debts (i.e., commingling)
     - Fails to keep separate corporate books
     - Fails to follow corporate protocols (i.e., filings, meetings, issuance of stock, and conducting business by resolution)

Does a Company Guarantee Asset Protection?

Must prevent "piercing of the corporate veil"

2) Undercapitalization
- No absolute test, but company should have enough capital to pay debts as they come due
- Put at risk unencumbered capital reasonably adequate for the company's prospective liabilities
- Consider scope of contemplated operations and the potential liability foreseeable from the company's operations
- Cannot prove solely by showing that the company is now insolvent (however, insolvency occurring shortly after incorporation may be a primary indicator of undercapitalization)

Does a Company Guarantee Asset Protection?

Must prevent "piercing of the corporate veil"

3) Fraud
- When avoidance of personal liability (through formation of a company) operates as a fraud on creditors/other third parties
- Actual intent to defraud is not always necessary—constructive fraud and avoiding an inequitable result is often enough
- Creating or dissolving a corporation to defraud creditors or other third parties
  - Example: X has covenant not to compete with Y, X cannot avoid covenant by forming a corporation and having it compete with Y

Does a Company Guarantee Asset Protection?

Areas of personal exposure

- Positions
    - Corporate officers and directors
    - LLC managers; LP/LLP general partners
- Personal actions or omissions
    - Illegal, fraudulent, negligent
- Personal guarantees
- Dividends/distributions made in violation of law

Separate Corporation Assets/Operations

- Way to avoid having liabilities take down the entire business
- Parent/subsidiary or affiliate structure
- Decide which fences to build
    - Geographic, lines of business
    - Asset types (real property, equipment, intellectual property)
- Respect your own fences (i.e., don't pierce corporate veil)
- Issues: corporate, employment, tax, accounting, logistics

Selecting the Right Form of Entity

Types of Entities

C corporations
S corporations
Limited liability companies (LLC)
Partnerships (LP, LLP)

Prepared by Snell & Wilmer LLP, for the Arizona Center for Innovation 15

Selecting the Right Form of Entity

	C Corp	S Corp	LLC	LP/LLP
Liability protection for owners	✓	✓	✓	✓ (not GP)
Single level of tax	Corporate and shareholder	✓	✓	✓
No restrictions on types of owners	✓	US persons / trusts	✓	✓
No limit on number of owners	✓	100-person limit	✓	✓

Prepared by Snell & Wilmer LLP, for the Arizona Center for Innovation 16

Selecting the Right Form of Entity

	C Corp	S Corp	LLC	LP/LLP
Different classes of ownership interests	✓		✓	✓
Can raise capital	✓	✓	✓	✓
Can raise venture or institutional capital	✓		✓ (depends)	✓ (funds)
Can do an IPO and be a publicly traded company	✓	✓ (if revoke S status)		

Selecting the Right Form of Entity

	C Corp	S Corp	LLC	LP/LLP
Can avoid self-employment tax	✓	✓	?	IRC 1402(a)13
Does not require pro rata distributions	But can do preferred stock		✓	✓
Can grant tax-free ownership interests			✓ (profits interest)	✓ (profits interest)
No annual filing requirements			✓	✓ (LLP files)

Selecting the Right Form of Entity

	C Corp	S Corp	LLC	LP/LLP
Flexible management structure			✓	
Can have incentive stock options (ISOs)	✓	✓		
Can have nonqualified equity options	✓	✓	✓ (no historic value)	✓ (no historic value)
Can have phantom stock/stock appreciation rights	✓	✓	✓	✓

Selecting the Right Form of Entity

Can you convert one type of entity into another <u>after</u> formation?

<u>Potentially</u>, but there could be a significant tax consequence

How to Form an Entity

	C Corp	S Corp	LLC	LP/LLP
Check name availability	✓	✓	✓	✓
Prepare and file:	Articles of incorporation; Certificate of Disclosure	Articles of incorporation; Certificate of Disclosure	Articles of Organization	Certificate of Partnership
Publish notice	✓	✓	✓	LLPs only
Obtain EIN	✓	✓	✓	✓
Prepare internal governing documents:	Bylaws; Board Consent; Stock Subscription and Certificates; Shareholders' Agreement	Bylaws; Board Consent; Stock Subscription and Certificates; Shareholders Agreement	Operating Agreement	Partnership Agreement
File S election		✓		

Template Forms

Template forms to assist in forming a corporation or LLC are provided by the Arizona Corporation Commission:

www.azcc.gov/divisions/corporations/filings/forms/index.asp

Template forms to assist in forming a limited partnership are provided by the Arizona Secretary of State:

www.azsos.gov/business_services/partnerships/PartnershipForms.htm

Owners' Agreements

- Stockholders' agreement
- Operating agreement
- Partnership agreement
- Regardless of the form of entity, governing documents generally address following topics, among others:
  - Different classes of equity
  - Who makes decisions? Who has authority?
  - Voting rights
  - Restrictions on transfer of equity
  - Rights of First Refusal/Co-Sale Rights

Recordkeeping

Corporate Minute Book
- Articles/Bylaws/Owners' Agreements
- Meeting Minutes/Actions by Written Consent
- Stock Ledger
- Material Agreements
- Annual Reports

LLC/Partnership Minute Book
- Articles of Organization/Certificate of Limited Partnership
- Operating Agreement/Partnership Agreement
- Annual Reports (Partnerships Only)

Capitalizing Your New Company

Who provides a new business with its initial capital?

The founder(s)

Capitalizing Your New Company

Who provides a new business with its next round of capital?

The founder(s)
and/or
their family and friends

Capitalizing Your New Company

Other sources of capital:

Angel investors (individual or organized groups)

Foundations/incubator and accelerator programs

Commercial banks

Government

(SBA loan, Small Business Innovation Research (SBIR) and Small Business Technology Transfer Research (STTR) grants, community development)

Comply with Securities Laws

Why? Failure to comply can ...

- Cause the investment to be unwound (rescission rights)

- Impact your ability to raise capital in the future

- Impact or even prevent the ultimate sale of the company

- Impact your ability to finance future companies

- Result in civil and criminal penalties for the company and its principals

When Are the Securities Laws Triggered?

When 1 share of stock is offered or sold to 1 person

What Laws Are Triggered?

1) Federal

2) State in which company is located

3) State in which investor is located

  * Do <u>not</u> assume uniformity

The Basic Rule

All securities offerings must be either:

1) Registered, or

2) Subject to an exemption from registration

Registered Offering	Exempt Offerings
Initial public offering (IPO) Secondary offerings	Security exemption Transaction exemption

The Basic Rule—Exempt Offerings

Security Exemption	Transaction Exemption
(Section 3(a) of Securities Act) Securities issued by government, banks, nonprofits Securities exchanged by issuer with existing security holders exclusively where no remuneration is paid (recap)	(Sections 3(a)(11), 3(b), 4(2) and 4(6) of Securities Act) Private offerings

The "Founders Exemption"

<u>Federal Exemption</u>

<u>Section 4(2)</u>
Transactions by an issuer not involving any public offering

<u>Arizona Exemption</u>
<u>AARS 44-1844(10)</u>
Issuance of securities to up to 10 original incorporators, if

- securities are not acquired for the purpose of sale to others
- securities are not sold to a third party within 24 months (unless an incorporator experiences a bona fide change of financial circumstances)

What Does It Mean to Have Partners?

<u>The rules you learned in kindergarten now apply:</u>

- Share management and economic rights
- Play fair and be mindful of fiduciary duties
- Don't hit people ... figuratively (or literally!)
- Say you are sorry when you hurt somebody
- Don't take things that aren't yours (like profits, credit for success)
- Look both ways before you cross the street (i.e., plan before you act)
- Follow the Golden Rule - treat partners like you want them to treat you

How Do You Bring Partners into the Business?

1) Discuss your vision for the company. Make sure they share your vision … and commitment to it

2) Discuss and agree upon the "rules of the game" (i.e., management and economic rights)

3) Hire a lawyer to accurately and completely capture those rules in a shareholders or operating agreement

4) Review and have each partner actually sign the shareholders' or operating agreement

And conduct a proper private offering if investment is part of the deal

Basic Agreements Every Business Must Have

- Equity purchase agreement (founders and all other investors)
- Shareholders or operating agreement (if more than one owner)
- Equity option or grant agreement (if applicable)
- Confidentiality, noncompetition, non-solicitation, assignment of inventions agreement (for everyone working for the company)
- Confidentiality agreement (for sharing proprietary information)
- Offer letter, employee handbook, employment agreement
- Independent contractor agreement
- Customer agreement
- Supplier/vendor agreement

Summary of Objectives

- Understand the advantages and disadvantages of the different types of entities available for your business and the appropriate entity or entities for you based on your business objectives.

- Understand the most common mistakes that a business owner may make in attracting personal liability with respect to the operation of his or her business.

- Understand the critical contractual agreements that a business owner should consider at the commencement of any business operations.

Follow-up Discussion/Action

If you haven't yet done so, what type of entity will you form and what steps will you take to ensure proper governance?

Assess your team and partner structure. What steps have you taken to pursue the right partnerships, and do you have the right agreements in place?

Review the agreements list and create a plan of action to address any missing documents that may be appropriate for your venture.

Arizona Center for Innovation Resources

Tools to help new companies navigate the incubation process

This chapter addresses three resources provided by the Arizona Center for Innovation and is aimed at new technology ventures:

1. The Innovation Continuum. Visually represents the chain of processes that happen from idea to success. This overlaps a company's stage of development, growth, and funding and is a keystone for ongoing program assessment and development for the Arizona Center for Innovation.

2. Program Overview and Milestones. Provides a table of critical elements that every new venture must address and identifies key milestones for each, as the company moves through the Innovation Continuum. This creates a checklist or a road map for both the incubator and the new venture, providing a unique and focused experience for each new venture.

3. Resource List. Provides resources, tips, links, and books that have been referenced throughout the workbook. These resources change constantly so refer back to our website for updates.

1. Innovation Continuum

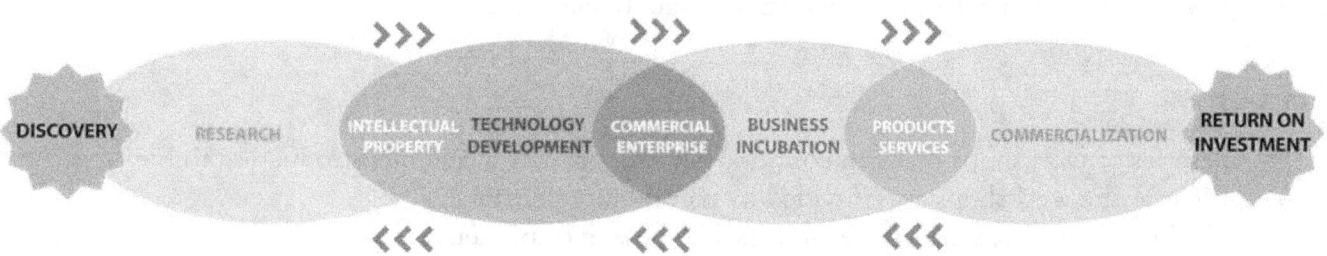

The Innovation Continuum © 2003, Arizona Board of Regents

The Innovation Continuum refers to the chain of activity that happens between discovery and return on investment, which may represent commercialization success; financial success; or other depending on the technology and objectives.

This is not a linear process; each link in the chain creates movement back and forth as the concept is assessed and modified. In some cases, the entrepreneur may start with a problem-solution-customer equation that does not change through this process, but the end result uses technology other than what was initially discovered. In other cases, the opposite is true - the end result may be the same technology with new applications.

Business incubation typically takes place once a technology concept prototype is tested, and the incubator team helps the entrepreneur or inventor build the business elements around the technology to carry it forward into commercialization. Once successfully in the market, the company will typically graduate from the incubator and continue to move forward in the community.

Unlike many other business incubators, the Arizona Center for Innovation (AzCI) provides programs designed for researchers who may still be in the earlier stages of research and technology development. AzCI supports the University of Arizona, and works closely with the McGuire Center for Entrepreneurship and the Office of Technology Transfer to provide a seamless connection for those researchers or new graduates who wish to bring their innovative ideas in to the community. AzCI also supports those inventors and entrepreneurs in the local community who are keen to successfully launch their new ventures. This combination of University and community effort creates a unique and dynamic experience that further sparks new ideas and opportunities. Instead of focusing just on the business incubation link as shown above, AzCI offers a range of programs that span from early research (pre-incubation) through to return on investment.

If you have any questions or would like to know more, please contact the Arizona Center for Innovation at www.azinnovation.com.

2. Program Overview and Milestones

The Arizona Center for Innovation offers a four-phase program that overlaps the Innovation Continuum: Start-up, Mentored Launch, Commercial Reality, and Tenant Track.

Start-Up

- » A series of workshops that run continuously and provide a general introduction to business.
- » Most of the workshops are provided by community partners.
- » Ideal for inventors, scientists, engineers, and new entrepreneurs.

Mentored Launch

- » Pre-incubation support, up to three months in length but varies with venture needs.
- » Services include: workshops, online content, and coaching.
- » Ideal for entrepreneurs who need early-stage assessment and preparation for incubation support.

Commercial Reality

- » Full incubation support, typically up to two years but varies with venture needs.
- » Services include: individual mentoring, coaching, workshops, executive sessions, support in creating an Advisory Committee and Board of Directors, industry contacts, University of Arizona interns, full-service work space, and discounted lab space. At the end of this phase, clients should be ready to graduate and move into community.

Tenant Track

- » Post-incubation support.
- » Services include: executive office space and access to lab space and equipment, managed on a company-by-company basis.
- » Ideal for those companies that no longer need incubation services but may not yet be ready to step into the community as full graduates.

On the table below, you will find a series of business elements in the left column and the first three program phases across the top. This is a foundational concept; for each business element, you will see the progression of knowledge and expertise typically experienced through incubation.

Every venture approaches this process differently based on their own strengths and weaknesses. Use this as a checklist for self-assessment and to help you create a plan to move forward. In this case, AzCI will use this to help with your initial assessment for admission to the incubator and will use this as a tool to measure your progress and success as you move along the Innovation Continuum.

Business Elements	Start-Up Phase	Mentored Launch Phase	Commercial Reality Phase
Business Presentation	Draft elevator pitch and presentation outline	Refined pitch (1, 2, 5 min), presentation, draft executive summary, business plan, draft mission/vision statement, and plan for name, domain, email, etc.	Refined pitch, presentation, executive summary and business plan, mission/vision statement, and secured name, domain, email, etc.
Problem	Understanding of: real customer problem vs. product/service ability	Define problem and alternative solutions, clearly state problem (< 25 words)	Completed and applied research to validate problem-solution-customer
Customer	Understanding of: difference between customer and end user	Define customers affected by problem and identify first 5 - 10 customers by name	Customer validation and written testimonials with alpha and best customers assigned
Solution	Understanding of general idea and application	Clearly state problem, alternatives, your solution, and connect problem, solution, customer	Customer validation and written testimonials, with plan to incorporate customer feedback continuously
Technology	Understanding of value proposition, IP options, development issues	Concept test, feasibility/validation done, identified prototype and testing plan, IP strategy and action plan drafted and in progress	Development plan in place, continued execution of IP strategy and action plan with broader IP portfolio
Alternate Valuation	Not always introduced at this phase, depends on venture concept	General discussion that concept may provide social, environmental, or other value beyond conventional finance and economic measures	Identified and measured alternate value and applicability to venture growth and sustainability; may include community or social responsibility, depending on venture
Business Model	Understanding of: competitor business models and how the company will sell and make money	Initial product pricing and sales plan, along with a draft business/economic model that will be tied to financials	A clear business/economic model fully integrated into rest of business plan
Scope and Scale	General introduction of "crusade" vs. "company" concepts and definition of scalable, innovative idea suitable for incubation support	Clarification of true concept, opportunity and application; typically a go vs. no-go decision point to continue venture and/or continue incubation services	Deep dive on concept, opportunity, and application; typically a key decision point in determining what next steps to take for venture development

Business Elements	Start-Up Phase	Mentored Launch Phase	Commercial Reality Phase
Industry, Environment, Legal, Governance	An understanding of: industry and environmental influences, barriers to entry, regulation and risk, and corporate governance	Early industry assessment and identification of regulations or perceived requirements. Note: required for next step: company formation and operating agreements, insurance, legal coverage, reporting plan for AzCI	Clear structure and protection in place: legal; insurance; regulation; etc. Ongoing reporting to AzCI Board of Directors in place
Competitive Advantage	An understanding of: top competitors and building a competitive advantage	Competitor analysis and comparison to venture, along with identified competitive advantages	Clear competitor differentiation and (sustainable) competitive advantages, a plan to follow competitive landscape and identified benchmark companies
Market Assessment	An understanding of market, market size, and a draft research plan	A revised research plan with key questions; secondary research should be near completion, and primary research should be in progress	Plan for ongoing market assessment
Sales and Marketing	An understanding of relevant sales and marketing strategies and how they connect	Draft go-to market and sales plans, including: branding, PR, marketing, sales. First customers and benchmark companies identified. Some knowledge of industry sales statistics	Established go-to market and sales plans, with initial marketing materials. By the end of this phase, the venture should have revenue or meaningful progress
Operations	An understanding of startup operations, make vs. buy decisions, etc.	A draft operations plan relevant to the business (QC, mfr, fulfillment and distribution, facilities, etc.)	A relevant and concise operations plan
Team	An understanding of key startup roles and how to work with incubator, advisors/mentors, and virtual teams	Assess team needs, create plan for management team with org chart, and plan for Advisory Committee	Developed team with industry/start-up experience, extended advisor team with tech/industry expertise, and Board of Directors
Financials	An understanding of: financial statements, P&L, cash flow, balance sheets	Draft financial statements (years TBD)	Final financial statements (3-5 yr), current operating financials, and plan for accounting/related services

Business Elements	Start-Up Phase	Mentored Launch Phase	Commercial Reality Phase
Funding considerations	An introduction to the funding process and general types of funding available	Draft fund strategy with a focus on early-stage funding to include founder investment and grants. Some discussion regarding fund options, valuation, term sheets	Successfully negotiated and secured initial funding, with follow-on funding strategy and exit strategy plans
Appendices	An introduction to the need for record keeping and version control of key company and technology documentation	Outline of due diligence materials needed, beginning archives for company documents	Secure archive of company documents, files, prototype materials, due diligence materials, etc.
Global Development	Provides support for two groups: young foreign companies that wish to build presence in the U.S. and those new U.S. companies that are keen to develop a global or international presence	Plan of action depends on company needs	Appropriate country entity formation, corporate governance, local regulation and IP protection, product localization and translation, manufacturing and distribution operations, regional sales and marketing plan, and secured local presence/resources

3. Great Resources

- » Abrams, Rhonda. *Business Plan in a Day: Get It Done Right, Get It Done Fast!*
- » Abrams, Rhonda. *Successful Business Plan: Secrets & Strategies (Successful Business Plan Secrets and Strategies).*
- » Burke, Barbara. *The Napkin The Melon & The Monkey: How to Be Happy and Successful by Simply Changing Your Mind.*
- » Christensen, Clayton M. *The Innovator's Dilemma: The Revolutionary Book that Will Change the Way You Do Business* (Collins Business Essentials).
- » Collins, Jim. *Good to Great: Why Some Companies Make the Leap … and Others Don't.*
- » Cottrell, David, Alice Adams, Juli Baldwin. *Monday Morning Leadership: 8 Mentoring Sessions You Can't Afford to Miss.*
- » Drummond, James H. *Marketing's 10 Deadly Sins (and How to Avoid Them).*
- » Gitomer, Jeffrey. Jessica McDougall, Paul "Doc" Hersey. *Jeffrey Gitomer's Little Book of Leadership: The 12.5 Strengths of Responsible, Reliable, Remarkable, and Resilient Leaders.*
- » Gitomer, Jeffrey. Jessica McDougall, Rachel Russotto. *Jeffrey Gitomers Little Red Book of Sales Answers: 99.5 Real World Answers That Make Sense, Make Sales, and Make Money.*
- » Gitomer, Jeffrey. *The Little Platinum Book of Cha-Ching.*
- » Gladwell, Malcolm. *Blink: The Power of Thinking Without Thinking.*
- » Gladwell, Malcolm. *The Tipping Point: How Little Things Can Make a Big Difference.*
- » Gladwell, Malcolm. *What the Dog Saw: And Other Adventures.*

» Godin, Seth. *Purple Cow, New Edition: Transform Your Business by Being Remarkable.*

» Godin, Seth. *Tribes: We Need You to Lead Us.*

» Kawasaki, Guy. *The Art of the Start: The Time-Tested, Battle-Hardened Guide for Anyone Starting Anything.*

» Kim, W. Chan. Renee Mauborgne. *Blue Ocean Strategy: How to Create Uncontested Market Space and Make Competition Irrelevant.*

» Lewis, Jim. *Five Deadly Sins CEOs Make in Sales.*

» Lencioni, Patrick. *The Five Temptations of a CEO, 10th Anniversary Edition: A Leadership Fable (J-B Lencioni Series).*

» McKinley, Mac. *Marketing Alignment: Breakthrough Strategies for Growth and Profitability.*

» Moore, Geoffrey A. *Crossing the Chasm.*

» Moore, Geoffrey A. *Inside the Tornado: Strategies for Developing, Leveraging, and Surviving Hypergrowth Markets (Collins Business Essentials).*

» Osterwalder, Alexander. Yves Pigneur. *Business Model Generation: A Handbook for Visionaries, Game Changers, and Challengers.*

» Schramm, Carl J. *The Entrepreneurial Imperative: How America's Economic Miracle Will Reshape the World (and Change Your Life).*

» Thorpe, Scott. *How to Think Like Einstein: Simple Ways to Break the Rules and Discover Your Hidden Genius.*

» Treacy, Michael. Fred Wiersema. *The Discipline of Market Leaders: Choose Your Customers, Narrow Your Focus, Dominate Your Market.*

FIRST Steps

Strategy for new technology
ventures by Joann MacMaster

What is FIRST

FIRST is a methodology designed to help early-stage technology companies organize and structure their plans for venture creation and first product launch. It stands for: Funding, Implementation, Resources, Sales and marketing, and Technology.

As an entrepreneur, it's easy to focus on the immediate and obvious need of funding to start your business. With the right capital you can then execute a plan, gather resources, and sell your product. This is a challenging strategy, however, as most investors typically look for the reverse to happen: initial customers or market traction with a working prototype where possible, engaged resources including an experienced and confident team, and other investment in the business (such as personal investment and grants).

There are many great strategic tools available. Use the FIRST method as a supplemental tool to help you sort out plans, identify and assign tasks, discuss issues with your team, and build a strategy that makes sense for your business.

How It Works

Flip the FIRST acronym around; draw it out over time, establish key milestones, and work backwards to create your plan. Following is an example of what this might look like on a timeline. You'll see the corresponding categories on the left, in reverse order of FIRST: Technology, Sales and marketing, Resources, Implementation, and Funding. Across each row you'll see corresponding tasks that need to be done over time, and you can easily identify the relationships between each task. Across the top you'll see actual dates. You want to be as specific as possible when you lay this out; actual dates give you actual deadlines, as well as credibility with your team, customers, and investors. Again, this is an example, and you may have other tasks and assignments specific to your venture. Depending on your project, that launch date may happen in three months or ten years - so try to put the timeline together as it fits your venture.

Each section is discussed below. This works best in a group brainstorming session; invite your Advisory Committee members or incubator team to participate.

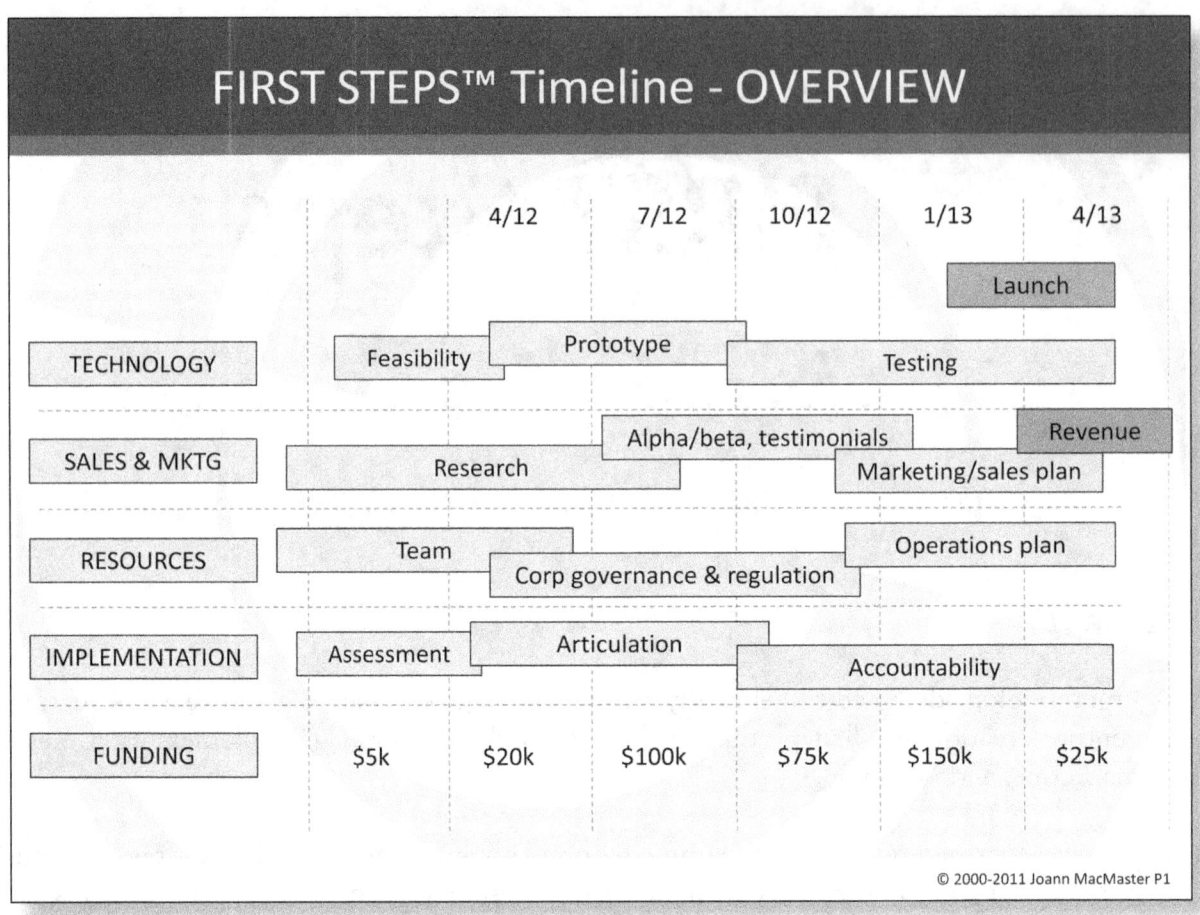

Technology

Why start with technology first? After all, you are the content expert and may have a great understanding of what it will take to bring your product to market. However, it's important to understand that all of these pieces interact and fit together to make a successful venture. In many cases, you'll need a concept representation or prototype to attract resources: partnerships, team members, investors, and so on. Consider the following:

1. Put a stake in the ground. Set a product release date based on an industry or customer event. It may change, but you need to start somewhere to start working backwards. This will help you proactively drive company growth and focus on the goal. As you go through the FIRST exercise, this date may change based on additional tasks and requirements, and that's OK. These are all moving parts, and once you're done with the full exercise, you should have a sense of how to move forward.

2. Can you develop what users want? Test your concept; is it feasible to develop? Can you document specifications and features from your customers' perspective?

3. Create a plan to secure intellectual property. You'll also want to build layers with patents, trade secrets, copyrights, trademarks, and registered trademarks. This helps you build a competitive advantage.

4. Create a development schedule and identify needs and resources.

5. Build out your prototype and testing plan. You'll need to establish alpha and beta customers and solicit and incorporate feedback and testimonials. Make sure to get permission before publishing those testimonials. Notice on the chart below that testing goes through launch.

6. Create a post-launch Bridge Plan that includes long-term testing, feedback, further development, product updates, and customer support services.

In the example below, the launch date was set for April 2013, and the key tasks were identified by working backwards. The level of detail and items will vary based on your technology needs. As your team visualizes this over time, think about the corresponding technology tasks and how they fit on the timeline. Save this work; you'll come back to this diagram when you bring all of the elements together.

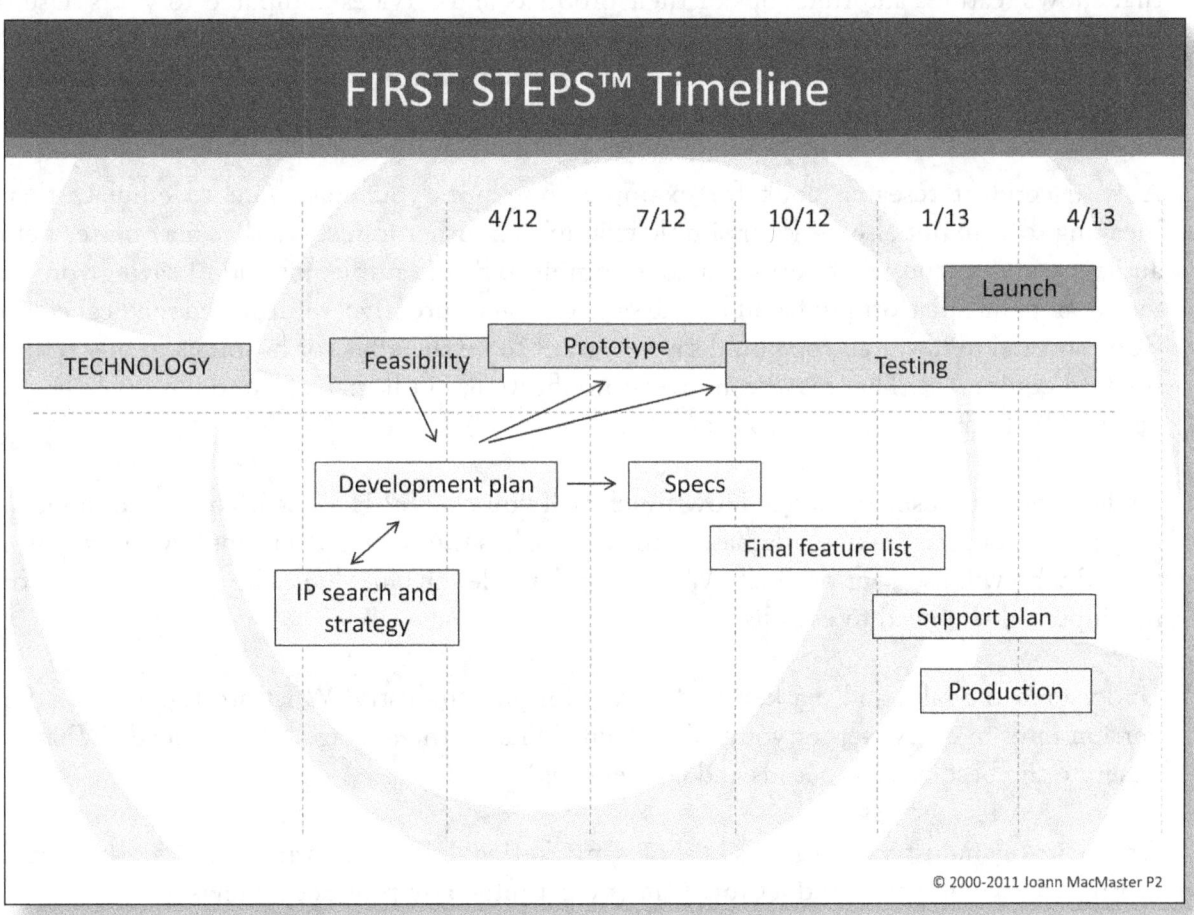

Sales and Marketing

At the *same time* you are building your technology plans, you should be considering your plans for sales and marketing. There are many overlaps; getting customers engaged early in the development and testing of your product can provide an invaluable resource for product validation, feedback, feature definition, and of course testimonials (positive feedback that you can use to help educate and promote your product in the market). Finding those initial customers requires some early preparation work, and here are a few things to consider:

1. Start with a research plan. Put together key questions for your business, and identify primary and secondary market research sources. For example, who will buy this product and why? Is this a growing market need? Does your solution fit the problem better than anything else available? What makes your product unique? How much is your customer willing to spend? How will you track market changes and trends?

2. Understand your competition. What alternative solutions exist today? If you had to identify the top two or three market competitors, who would they be and why? Create a comparison grid that shows features and functions of their products and services compared to yours. Use this to help identify weaknesses as well as new opportunities. Note: identifying your competitors is also a strategic action. It may set the pace of your company, identify new partner and customer opportunities, and drive your product development.

3. As you conduct research, look for example companies you may want to emulate that have meaning to you. But also look for simple examples in other industries that may better help your audience understand what you want to accomplish. For example, instead of saying you are providing an online platform to facilitate the sale of capital-intensive, refurbished medical equipment from hospital to hospital, you could say you want to be the eBay for hospitals to buy refurbished medical equipment. That may be an oversimplification, but it may serve to illustrate the point so you set the frame of mind for your audience.

4. Understand the business model. How much will you charge? How will you make money? How long does it take to make a purchase, and who makes the buying decisions? Who are you selling to, and who will use your product? What does that sales channel look like, and what kind of partnerships will you need to establish?

5. Understand the sales and marketing dynamic for your industry. What are the averages for conversion rates in every step of your sales chain? What is the average cost per lead? What sources generate the best customer leads and conversions?

6. Are there key industry events - trade shows, marketing or PR events and the like - that you'll need to prepare for and need product for? Can you get into early product reviews?

7. Establish your marketing strategy based on research and create your corresponding tactical plan, but track the success of each action so that you can adjust your tactics accordingly. Do the same for your sales plan.

8. Who are your top five to ten customers? Can you name them?

9. Do you have an opportunity for ongoing revenue (support, add-ons, etc.)?

Consider how these projects overlap with the technology piece on your FIRST timeline, and look at the relationships between the tasks:

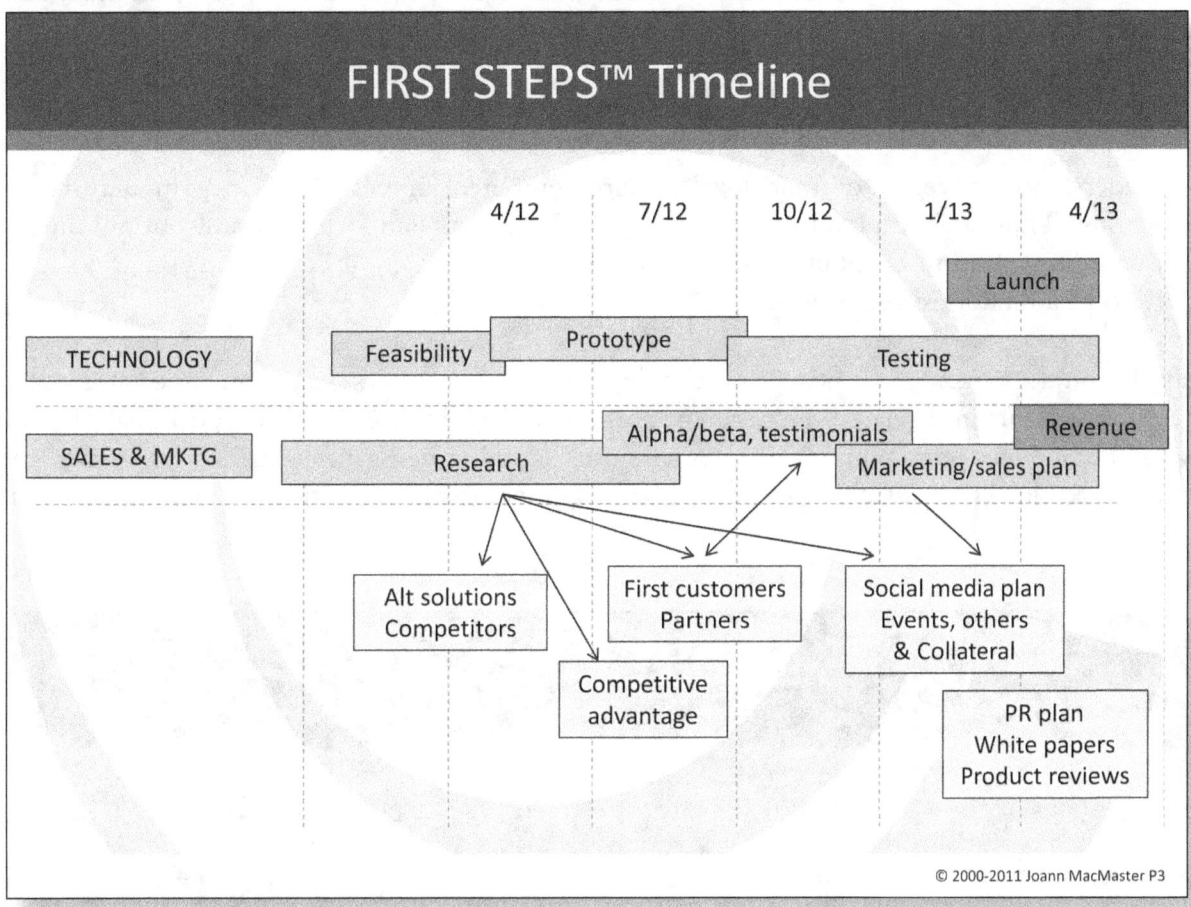

Resources

Now that you are building an outline of tasks associated with starting your venture and bringing your product to market, what resources are needed to help you accomplish those tasks successfully?

1. Start first with an assessment of your team - conduct a Strengths, Weaknesses, Opportunities, and Threats (SWOT) analysis to identify areas for focus and support.

2. Immediately identify and build an Advisory Committee. This should be a committee of experienced entrepreneurs, mentors, and industry experts that are engaged as volunteers in your company. Ask your incubator team for help in pulling together the right team and how to best manage, motivate, focus, inspire, and communicate with your Advisory Committee. The right mix of people with the right incentives can have a significant and positive impact on the success of your company.

3. Prepare to bring in a C-Team of executives, which may include a CEO. In many cases, you are the content expert but may not have experience successfully starting and growing new ventures. Strive to surround yourself with better, faster, stronger, smarter - create a dynamic powerhouse team that will help ensure success.

4. Create an organizational chart and understand what staffing needs you'll have and by when.

5. Create a Corporate Governance and Administration plan, and identify your goals and plans for a Board of Directors.

6. Research and identify your operations and manufacturing needs: facilities, equipment, etc.

7. Understand any regulatory and legal requirements, real or perceived, in your industry and/or market. Those might include regulation by the U.S. Food and Drug Administration; the International Organization for Standardization; the U.S. Environmental Protection Agency; the Underwriter Laboratories; and others.

Overlap this on the timeline as it fits with technology and sales and marketing. You'll see patterns begin to emerge as projects are interrelated. This is an important concept for consideration. Although this timeline is linear and based on a fixed point of time, you'll note that the process is not linear. You need to consider all of these variables at the *same time* - a compelling argument to engage with an incubator early and build a strong team.

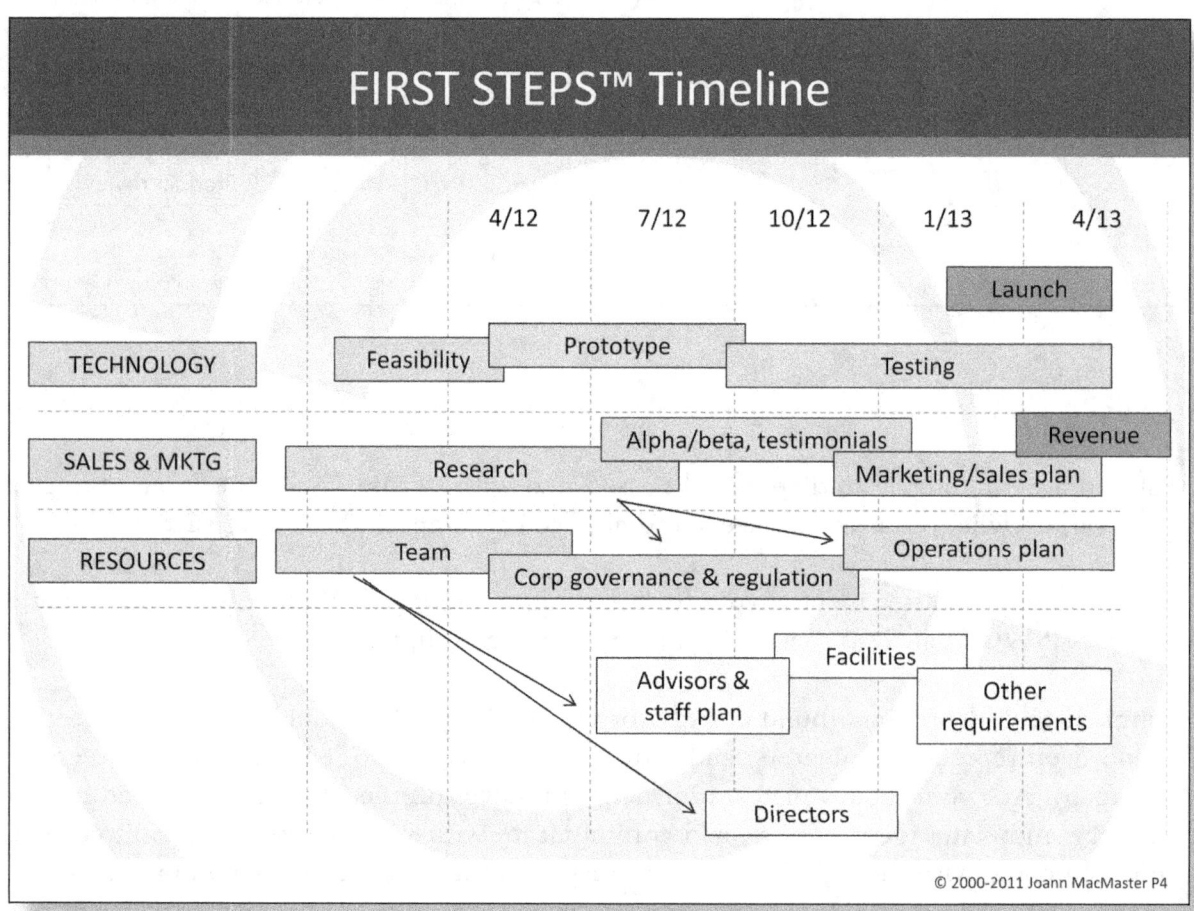

© 2000-2011 Joann MacMaster P4

Implementation

This is the final piece in pulling everything together. Having a plan is not enough; you need to have a plan for execution and accountability. Here are some things to consider:

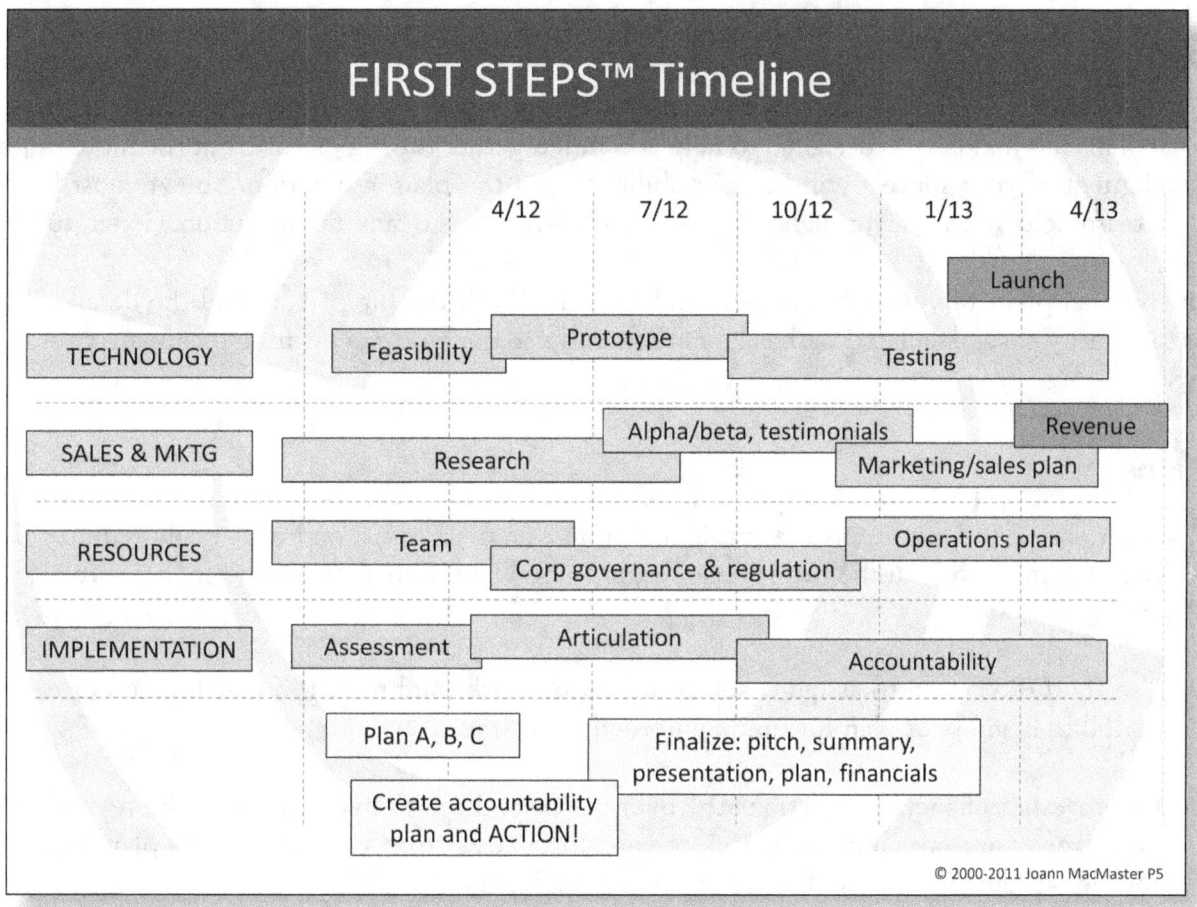

1. Pull together all timelines, milestones, and outstanding issues from the FIRST plan to assess venture needs, reassess the timeline, and prioritize tasks. Remember to keep your tasks in small, bite-sized pieces and don't let your team be overwhelmed with the big picture.

2. Formulate Plan A, Plan B, Plan C, and maybe even Plan D. What can realistically be accomplished with the resources available? How does this impact your time to market, and how fundable is your business? Do the risks vary with each plan?

3. Create an accountability plan. Establish time-specific metrics that help you measure progress and identify areas of change. Have your incubator team or your Advisory Committee help you hold that accountability to stay focused and ensure the company moves forward.

4. Build revenue projections. Identify product price, sales process and margins, first customers, and keep year-over-year growth realistic. Do you have other revenue streams in addition to product

sales (support, add-ons, etc.)? If so, include those in your projections as a separate revenue line item.

5. Start working on your business presentation and investor materials. That includes: the elevator pitch, executive summary, investor presentation, business plan and any supporting documentation.

6. Start working on your financial models for cash flow, income statement, and balance sheet.

7. IMPLEMENT, EXECUTE, TAKE ACTION. If this were easy, everyone would already have done it. This methodology is designed to help you pull together the big picture, but the more important element of your success will be your ability to put the plan into action. You've most likely had a team help you walk through this FIRST plan - you are already taking action. Congratulations!

This is the final piece to your timeline and pulls together both the big picture and the detail. The next step is to identify costs associated with each of these tasks so that you can begin to formulate your funding strategy.

Funding

This is often one of the first items for consideration in a start-up venture, but it really requires the rest of the plan to come into focus before you can begin to build a funding strategy. Here are some items for discussion:

1. Use the FIRST plan to assign costs to the various tasks and total those at the end of each time period to begin your plan for funding needed over time.

2. Pull together financial projections to cover the next three to five years. Use the revenue projections from your sales and marketing research, the costs from your operations plan, and identify additional startup costs as outlined on your FIRST plan.

3. You will likely show a yearly summary in your investor presentation and executive summary that includes revenue, costs, and EBITDA (Earnings Before Interest, Taxes, Depreciation, and Amortization), but you should have all notes and corresponding data in your supporting documentation. Your incubator may have a recommended financial template and mentors, partners, or staff who can help you create this.

4. Understand your total capital need. Remember to include not just the costs that appear on your FIRST plan, but also consider the operating costs required to reach break-even and whatever additional working capital you may need. Focus on cash flow.

5. Be prepared before you seek outside funding. Investors will want to see personal investment , often referred to as "skin in the game" from the founders. Your time is valuable, but they are primarily looking for your investment in terms of CASH. If you are able but have not invested in your own business, that's a big red flag for potential investors.

6. Consider personal investment through cash, loans, or investment from family and friends, and pursue whatever grant opportunities are available. Ask your incubator or Advisory Committee for ideas and recommendations. Your goal is to build as much momentum and traction as possible before seeking outside investment.

7. What is your company valuation? Once you have completed the financials and your plan, you can use that information to help determine your company valuation, an important step before you begin working with outside investors. Common valuation methods include: discounted cash flow, cost to recreate, market multiple, etc. More current methods also include the balanced scorecard, and stage of development, etc. Work with your incubator or Advisory Committee if you need help walking through this process.

8. Target appropriate investors. Consider their portfolio of investments and look for someone who may also be able to bring additional resources and support to your team.

Following is the example with costs associated to each project. These are samples - the tasks and amounts will vary and should be specific to your venture needs.

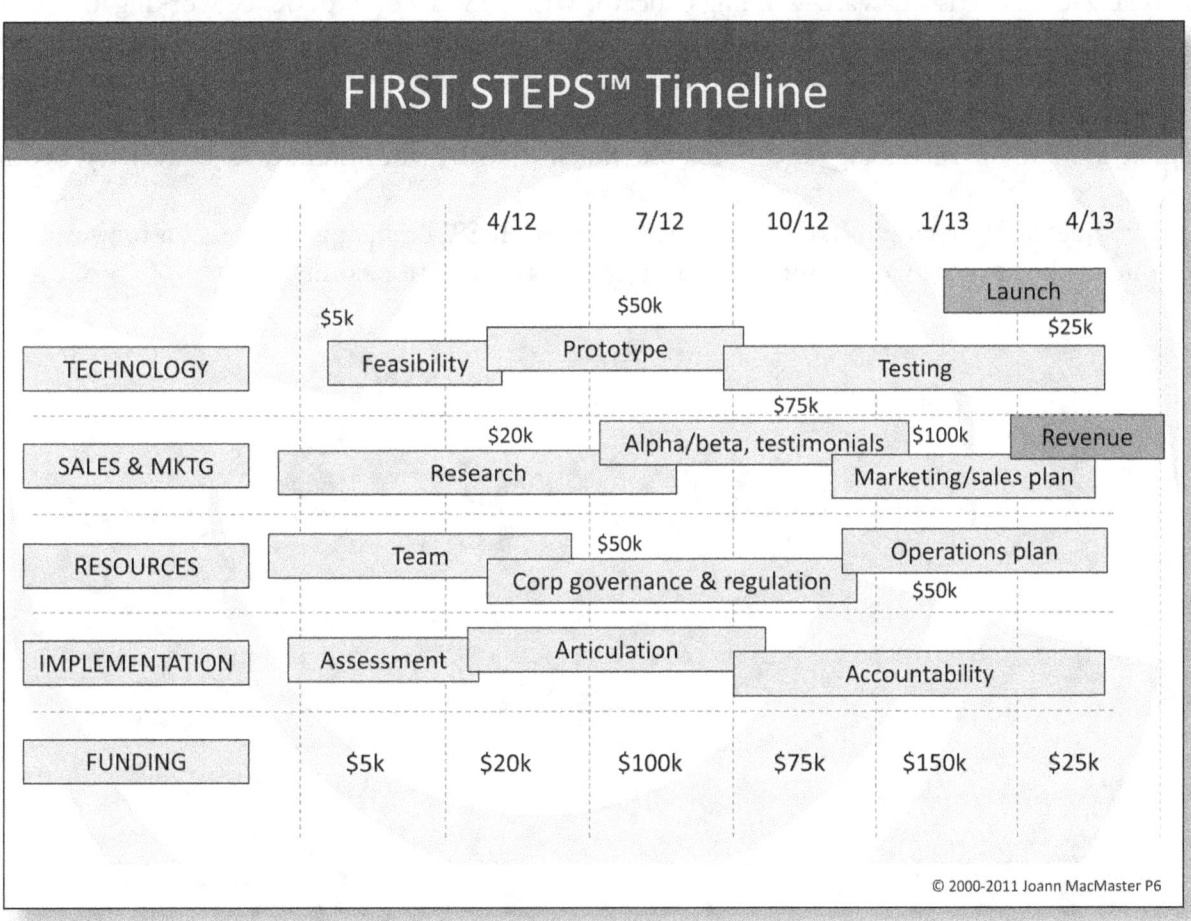

Summary

Use the FIRST method as a supplemental tool to help you sort out plans, identify and assign tasks, discuss issues with your team, and build a strategy that makes sense for your business.

If you don't yet have an Advisory Committee, use the FIRST strategy sessions as an opportunity to build one and engage them in discussion. You will gain early confidence and support from your extended team as you move your venture forward. Good luck!

About the FIRST STEPS™ TimeLine:

This methodology was created in 2000 by Joann Rockwell MacMaster as a framework to help track the progress of technology incubator clients. It has since been used by over two hundred technology startup companies and has been revised by the author for use in this publication.

Joann MacMaster is a successful hi-tech entrepreneur and board-level executive with over 20 years of experience in the areas of leadership, strategic planning, innovation, and new product development and commercialization. She is an award-winning educator with 10 years of experience working in higher education as a member of faculty, administration, and as an entrepreneur. She currently serves as Director of the Arizona Center for Innovation. Prior to this she served as President with Cortiva Institute, Program Director with the McGuire Center for Entrepreneurship at the University of Arizona, and VP Client Services at the Tucson Technology Incubator. She holds an MBA from Edinburgh University, Scotland.

If you have questions or would like help in facilitating a FIRST brainstorming session for your venture, please contact the Arizona Center for Innovation, www.azinnovation.com.

From Marketing Strategy to Action Plan

14

Supplement to FIRST Steps™ sales and marketing by Joann MacMaster

Strategy: Where to Start

If you are challenged to create your marketing strategy and corresponding plans and budgets, following are a few tips and examples that may help. This is a great exercise to work through with your team, and often uncovers issues in the process that you may not have otherwise considered.

Let's assume your early customer feedback and market research efforts validate your product/service. Your prospective customer has a true need, and you have the right solution; this is a true win-win! The challenge now becomes educating your customer on the value of your solution and creating a plan that spans the first few years of your business to ensure stability and growth. For example, a new venture's overall strategy might include the following goals (and these should be modified to be specific for your venture):

Build Credibility

» Build presence and acceptance in your market.
» Look at other companies you may wish to emulate (these may be your benchmark companies) and examine how they build credibility with their products and services. Can you take similar action and improve? As a side note, this does not necessarily mean to emulate those companies entirely. An important part of innovation is doing something new. A great resource for more information on this idea, we recommend: *Blue Ocean Strategy: How to Create Uncontested Market Space and Make Competition Irrelevant* by W. Chan Kim, Renee Mauborgne.
» Action: customer testimonials, PR and independent product reviews, recognized partnerships, regulation or accreditation approvals, right facility or location, etc.

Educate Market

» Capture mindshare, become a market leader, and help customers see your value proposition.

- » Become the go-to guru or voice of your industry that others look to for direction, advice, and ultimately decision support on purchasing (your) products and services; this also helps build credibility.
- » Action: PR and independent product reviews, white papers and editorials, training or education opportunities; workshops, tradeshows, interviews, agency or association participation, partners, and etc.

Engage the Customer

- » Engage your customer early in the development cycle. If you do this well, you will not only get great feedback and testimonials, but you will also get buy-in and a sense of ownership and pride from your customers. They will more likely refer your product and service to others and help you promote your business.
- » Find a good tool to record and track your customer information for follow-up. Some examples include: Salesforce.com, ACT!, Zoho, SugarCRM.
- » Action: conduct primary research through events, usability labs, feasibility discussions, alpha/beta testing, workshops and etc.

Execute—SELL!

- » Build your distribution channel – the partners or mechanism through which your product will reach the user.
- » Create new demand and increase your customer base – generate REVENUE!
- » Generate leads. Understand the sales process and the typical conversion rates (lead to sales) for your industry so that you can begin to understand and program key metrics like cost per lead, cost per sale, etc. This is critical to forming your marketing budget.
- » Generate leads, and you'll generate revenue!
- » Note: not everyone will buy your product or service - but everyone can become a referral.
- » Action: PR, website, direct marketing, events, advertising and promotion, social media, partners.

Strategy: The First Years for Stability and Growth

As noted above, the challenge is not just in educating your customer but in creating a plan that spans the first few years of your business to ensure stability and growth. For example, a new venture's strategy for the first years might include (these should be specific for your venture):

Year 1: Launch Product

- » Focus efforts on: PR; write white papers and editorials; build strategic partnerships and gather testimonials. Plan events for education, awareness, and product launch.
- » Possibly no marketing spend on traditional advertising.

Year 2: Build Presence

- » Increase marketing budget for partnerships, social media, and events; plan an advertising campaign.
- » Reprioritize if needed. In this example, assume the PR activities in the first year were successful, so shift the budget slightly to focus on the other areas.

» Be solid and consistent in your messaging and the look and feel, and realize that many traditional avenues (like print advertising) require longer commitments. However, where possible, be flexible and willing to adjust the budget accordingly.

Year 3: Stabilize

» Now with some awareness and presence, focus on stability and market dominance.
» Refine your marketing strategy and reprioritize if needed. In this example, assume a growth in social media and specialty events.
» Don't be complacent. Start looking for new partners, new markets, and new opportunities.

Year 4: Expand

» Reinvest your resources. If the company is cash-flow positive, make sure you are reinvesting in the right marketing areas, new product development, team growth, etc.
» Look for new opportunities. Once you have a foothold in a particular market, take that experience and success to a new market. Look for new technology builds, complementary technologies, and other ways to grow. One-hit wonders only ever work in the music business (and even then, not really).

These are just examples to illustrate how you might create your strategy over time. The timeline and milestones will change based on your technology, company dynamic, industry, and other variables. Use these examples to spark your own ideas. This is a great opportunity to bring together your team, advisors, mentors, and partners to brainstorm! Create a strategy and set of action plans that makes sense for *your* venture.

Once that's done, you're ready to take the next step.

Translate Strategy to Action

Pull together the content from both strategy sessions identified above. You should have action items tied to specific goals and objectives, and you'll want to identify those actions over time. It might be helpful to put this in a matrix. Include key actions and yearly objectives, and the fill in the specific items for each cell:

Action	Year 1: Launch	Year 2: Presence	Year 3: Stabilize	Year 4: Expand
PR	Number white papers Number editorials Number testimonials *Be specific and set goals. For example: 20 publications, 4 papers, 2 editorials, 7 customer testimonials … whatever is relevant for your venture goals. List the actual publications and papers you plan to pursue.*	Number white papers Number editorials Number new journalist contacts		

Action	Year 1: Launch	Year 2: Presence	Year 3: Stabilize	Year 4: Expand
Events	Number industry events Number workshops Number training sessions *As with above, set specific goals. Name and calendar the events; identify your objectives for each.*			
Social Media				
Advertising				
Partners				

Assign Costs and Track Success

The better your plan is, the better your ability to execute and be successful. It's also equally important to identify key goals and objectives and success measures for each of the items. These should be hard and fast numbers: leads generated from an event or ad or paper; product reviews, press releases, journalist relationships, partners, etc.

For example, let's say you were planning to launch a new consumer electronic device. One of your actions might be to exhibit at the annual international CES tradeshow. Your goal for the show might be to host a press room (to announce a new partnership, for example), meet with the corresponding press doing a product First Look, exhibit and showcase your product on the floor with promotional materials to generate interest and leads, speak at one of the breakout sessions, and attempt to catch the attention for the CNET Best of Show award. These are very specific actions and goals that can be measured. Take this a step further and specify event costs for financial accountability, budget building, and a measurable result that can be used to plan your next event. For example:

Action	Leads	Customers
Trade show Total budget: $100	50 leads expected Cost per lead: $2	5 new customers expected Cost per customer acquisition: $20 Conversion of lead to customer: 10%

This is a simple example, and you may need to insert steps in the process specific to your business. They could include sales partners or qualifying leads, for example. Compare this to benchmark companies, industry standards, and your own performance after the event and adjust your goals accordingly for the next trade show.

Understanding how you perform against those standards provides valuable insight on any changes you may want to make in your sales channel, where to spend your marketing dollars, what type of content and collateral you may need, and how to train your sales team.

Translate Action to Budget

There are many ways to build out a marketing budget: based on historical data, as a percentage of sales, based on industry benchmarks, etc. But these methods are difficult for a start-up company that may not have historical or specific industry data. Another idea may be to consider similar industries for a range of acceptable benchmarks as a starting point.

When thinking about sales, the best advice is to focus on those first five to ten customers rather than on gaining a percentage of market value. This is important, because it demonstrates credibility and traction, and it gives the venture a clear action plan of first steps to take. The same applies to marketing. Rather than base a budget on a percentage of sales or industry benchmarks (although it's valuable to consider), focus instead on those first few action items required to reach your audience. Be as clear and as specific as possible.

This is the foundation of your budget. Understanding these specific actions, over time, and their associated costs, helps you to pull together your budget. Once you have the actual costs in place over time, chart everything out so you can look for visual clues about trends, issues, and concerns, and then adjust accordingly.

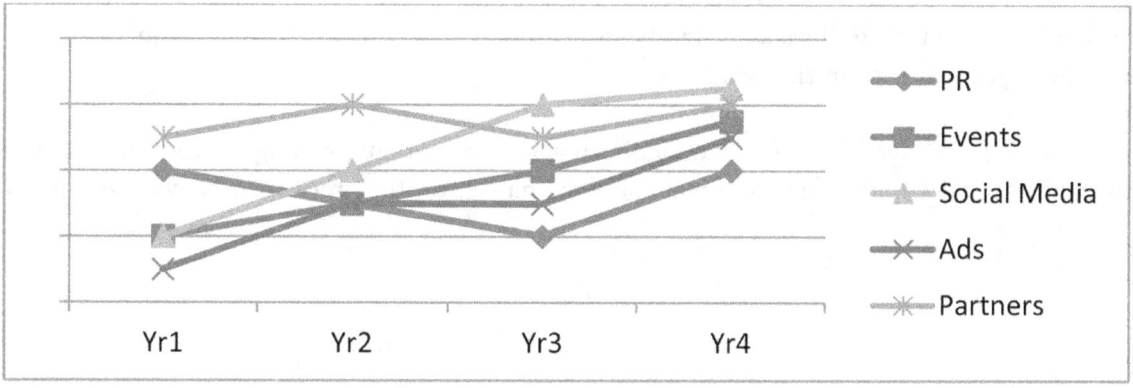

In this example, the action items mirror the yearly objectives, and it's easy to visually see the changing dynamic of the marketing plan over time. Give it your gut check - does it make sense for your venture? What questions does it raise with your team? Is this is a plan you can execute and measure success against?

Next Steps and Final Thoughts

Building a strategy for sales and marketing can be tricky. This is an area of the plan that most people are somewhat familiar with, but it requires clear direction, detail, and measurable results to succeed. Failure to strategically plan could have a devastating and long-lasting negative impact on your venture success.

Most important: don't fear the S-word (*sales*). If you have a great product and your prospective customer has a true need, then this becomes a win-win solution for everyone!

If you would like to learn a little more about sales and marketing, here are some handy resources:
http://www.gitomer.com/
http://www.sethgodin.com/sg/
http://planningshop.com/

About the FIRST Steps™ Sales and Marketing Handout:

This chapter is designed to help you manage the process of transitioning from strategy to tactical budget. It is a supplemental tool for use with the FIRST timeline, and is a great exercise to work through with your team as you formulate your initial business strategies. These sessions do focus on the 30,000-foot-view, which can be difficult when you face daily challenges in starting and growing your venture. However, they serve as a valuable compass to set, monitor, and adjust your course of action and often uncover issues that you may not have otherwise considered.

A quick tip and great habit to adopt is to set aside one day per month for administrivia. Skip the office and don't answer new email; instead use the day to focus on the little details, tasks and outstanding issues that you can't seem to conquer with your hectic schedule. Along these same lines, set aside one day per month to focus on the 30,000-foot-view. Use your extended team, and brainstorm some of these topics as a way to set or recalibrate that compass.

Strengthen your ability to telescope. As an entrepreneur, you will be tasked to keep one eye on the tiniest of tasks, with the other focused on the big picture. It's difficult to find balance, and your ability to shift focus between the two will make a significant difference. Setting aside fixed time, even one day per month, will help you strengthen that skill.

If you have questions or would like help in facilitating a FIRST brainstorming session for your venture on this or any of the FIRST topics, please contact the Arizona Center for Innovation, www.azinnovation.com.

Acknowledgments

The Arizona Center for Innovation is a community effort, and we would like to thank our valued partners, mentors, advisors, staff, and incubator companies for making our incubator such a great success!

Arizona Center for Innovation Team

To our immediate team, thank you for your continued passion, support, and commitment to every new venture we serve. You invest a large part of yourselves in the incubation process, recognized or not, and often your experience is just as intense as that of the individual founders. You are a true team of super-heroes, and we recognize, value, and appreciate your hard work.

» **Bruce Wright**, President, Arizona Center for Innovation, and Associate Vice President for University Research Parks, University of Arizona
» **Molly Gilbert**, Director of Community Engagement, University of Arizona, Office of University Research Parks
» **Joann MacMaster**, Director, Arizona Center for Innovation
» **Anita Bell**, Client Services Manager, Arizona Center for Innovation
» **Lori Kavanaugh**, Administrative Support, Arizona Center for Innovation

The University of Arizona, Office of University Research Parks Team

To our extended team, although some of your efforts happen "behind the curtain," please know that we recognize and appreciate your hard work, commitment, and dedication to both the incubator operations and the new ventures we serve. The incubator would not be a success without your help and support!

» **Diane Cardiel**, Department Administrator, Executive Assistant to Bruce Wright
» **Samantha Ellison**, Accountant
» **Bernadette Franco**, Executive Assistant and HR Coordinator
» **John Grabo**, Director of Business Development
» **Hilary Hirsch**, Business Development Coordinator
» **Craig Kleine**, IT Officer
» **Jaewon Lim**, Regional Economist and Intern Coordinator
» **Peter Loya**, Tenant & Employee Relations Coordinator
» **Ken Marcus**, Director, UA Tech Park, and CFO
» **Remi McKenzie**, Director of Facilities and Construction
» **Mark Rico**, Lab Coordinator, CH2M Hill
» **Jessa Turner**, Media and Public Relations Coordinator
» **Jim Weingart**, Accounting
» **Kathy Williams**, Support
» The CH2MHILL Team

Program Design Dream Team

To our dream program design team, thank you for your help and support in creating our Program Overview and Milestones table. This unique collaboration has led to new and relevant program content for the Arizona Center for Innovation, and to new opportunities for us to work together and better serve our community.

Curtis Gunn, Chairman, Desert Angels

» Curtis Gunn is Chairman of the Desert Angels, an angel investment group of 70 accredited investors in Tucson, Az. Prior to this role, Mr. Gunn traveled the world competing as a professional cyclist riding for both US and Australian-based Professional Cycling teams. Previous to his life as a professional athlete, he was an entrepreneur founding and operating companies based in retail, Internet, healthcare and real estate. As an angel investor, Curtis has invested in dozens of companies across a broad base of industries, technologies, and geographies.

Basil "Base" E. Horner, Screening Panel Chairman, Desert Angels

» Currently, Mr. Horner serves as an Executive Board Member and Chairman of the Screening Panel for the Desert Angels. He is a co-founder of Arch Partners LLC, a team of successful entrepreneur-investors who utilize their expertise in "go to market" strategy and execution, financing and exit strategies to build and realize value for the owners of their portfolio companies. He is a Senior Advisor to Cave Creek Capital Management, LLC, a private equity investor in middle market companies. In 1999, Mr. Horner was a co-founder of US Capital Partners LLC, a boutique investment banking firm formed to provide middle-market companies with advisory services. Prior to founding USCP, Mr. Horner spent three years as a Senior Managing Director in the Corporate Finance Division of EVEREN Securities, Inc. (subsequently, acquired by Wachovia Securities). From 1986 to 1996, Mr. Horner was employed at Smith Barney, Inc. as a Director in the Corporate Finance Division. Prior to Smith Barney, Mr. Horner was employed by First Interstate Bank of California as a Corporate Banking Officer where he was responsible for marketing and structuring senior credit products to clients. Mr. Horner received his Bachelor of Arts degree with honors in Business Economics from the University of California at Santa Barbara and a M.B.A. degree with honors in finance and marketing from the University of Chicago.

Sherry Hoskinson, Director, McGuire Center for Entrepreneurship, the University of Arizona and Co-director, Business / Law Exchange, the University of Arizona

» Sherry Hoskinson is the director of the University of Arizona's McGuire Center for Entrepreneurship, which houses a nationally top ranked entrepreneurship education program including formal degree program in entrepreneurship. Areas of focus have spanned design, planning, coordination, and implementation of the center's academic programs, including development of new venture/innovation teaching models for award winning McGuire Entrepreneurship Program; highly visible outreach and development, research and scholarship, entrepreneurship awareness and promotion activities, and activities to advance the discipline of entrepreneurship across local and national academic and business communities. Major initiatives include design and successful implementation of broad-based Technology Transfer Initiatives; Knowledge Transfer Initiative; Entrepreneurship and Innovation Initiative; Entrepreneurship/Law Exchange: the Mock Law Firm; Associates in Entrepreneurship Programs; Eller Scholars program; numerous elective courses and new tracks and concentrations in entrepreneurship across the University of Arizona campus.

Patrick L. Jones, Ph.D./MBA, Director, Office of Technology Transfer, the University of Arizona

» Dr. Jones directs The University of Arizona's Office of Technology Transfer, the unit that facilitates the movement of UA's leading-edge knowledge into new products and services. An expert in the business applications of intellectual property and new business development, Dr. Jones has extensive public and private sector work experience. In the public sector, Dr. Jones has held regular and affiliate faculty Chemistry appointments at major U.S. universities, managed University-Industry research and relations, and worked as a technology transfer specialist. In the private sector, he has directed product strategy and new business development for an Internet managed service provider, managed international marketing and sales for a manufacturer of solid-state laser and optical systems, and conducted research and product development for an aerospace contract research firm. He is a Past President and former Trustee of the Association of University Technology Managers (AUTM), the global association of academic technology transfer professionals. Dr. Jones holds an interdisciplinary Ph.D. in Chemical Physics from the University of Colorado Boulder's JILA Institute and a Masters in Business Administration from the University of Washington's Foster School of Business.

Tom Shambo, Director, Small Business Development Center

» Mr. Shambo currently serves as the Director of the Small Business Development Center where he has served for 5 years as a Business Analyst providing one-on-one counseling, resource assistance and training to support small businesses. Prior to joining the Small Business Development Center, Mr. Shambo led the information security team at CapGemini. He is a successful entrepreneur and business owner, with over 25 years of entrepreneurial experience as a consultant and software developer. He has a degree in Business Management from the University Bellevue, Nebraska and is a Certified Information Security Manager (CISM).

Justin Williams, Executive Emeritus, Arizona Technology Council

» Mr. Williams joined the Council and established the Tucson office as part of its 2008 merger with AMIT – Tucson's Aerospace, Manufacturing and Information Technology Cluster, where he served as founder and Executive Director since 2005. Prior to his tenure with the Council, Mr. Williams worked for over 10 years with high-tech firms in Southern Arizona including Electronic Data Systems, Intuit, and Ventana Medical Systems. He is the founder of StartupTucson.com. Justin Williams is a Ph.D. candidate in the MIS program at the University of Arizona, and from the same university holds a certificate from the McGuire Center for Entrepreneurship, a BS in Systems Engineering, and an MBA in Marketing and Finance. In 2011, Justin Williams was named as one of Tucson's "40-Under-40" by the Arizona Daily Star. He's been married to his wife Dawn for 13 years and is a father to his 4 year son J.J.

Content Contributors

We would like to thank our mentors and partners for their generous contributions of time and expertise to our incubator. For a complete list along with contact information and details, visit www.azinnovation.com. If you have any questions about this or would like to volunteer and join our team, please contact us.

Creating this workbook and the corresponding videos for our website has been a significant undertaking, and we would like to extend our gratitude to the following mentors, partners and incubator companies who volunteered their time to help us with this project:

- » Randy Accetta, Ph.D., Communications Mentor, McGuire Center for Entrepreneurship, University of Arizona
- » Anne Aikman-Scalese, Esq. of Counsel, Lewis and Roca LLP
- » Mark Banister, Founder and CTO, Medipacs, Inc.
- » Steve Bernat, Founder and CEO, RallyUp.com
- » Jim Butler, CEO and Founder, HJ3 Composite Technologies
- » Robert A. Fortuno, Esq., Attorney, Robert A. Fortuno P.C.
- » Rick Gibson, Managing Director, HOTventures
- » Sam Godin, Account Manager, Digital Dimensions Incorporated
- » George E, Henderson, CPA, BeachFleischman, PC
- » John J. Horn, Senior Intellectual Property Counsel, Raytheon Company
- » Ray Jacolik, Manager of Product Development and Operations, MSDx
- » Huw Jones, JD, MBA, Patent Counsel, Hayes Soloway, P.C.
- » Jan Knight, President, Bancroft Information Services, LLC
- » Sivan Korn, Esq., Partner, Lewis and Roca LLP
- » Eric B. Maneval, CPA, BeachFleischman, PC
- » Ramesh Nayak, Ph.D., Director of Research, MSDx
- » Eric Nielsen, Esq., Associate, Intellectual Property Group, Snell & Wilmer LLP
- » Kay Nelson, Esq., Shareholder, Haralson, Miller, Pitt, Feldman & McAnally, PLC
- » Quan Nguyen, Esq., Partner, Nguyen & Tarbet, PLLC
- » Mark Patton, Esq., Attorney, Lewis and Roca LLP
- » Angela Perez, Esq., Associate, Bus & Finance Group, and Chair of the Bioscience Industry Group, Snell & Wilmer LLP
- » Cynthia Pillote, Esq., Partner, Intellectual Property Group, Snell & Wilmer LLP
- » Joshua Scott, Director of Operations, bioVidria
- » Corey Smith, President and CEO, bioVidria
- » Matthew Sweger, Esq., Partner, Lewis and Roca LLP
- » Lowell Thomas, Esq., Partner, Business and Finance Group, Snell & Wilmer LLP
- » Emre Toker, Mentor in Residence, McGuire Center for Entrepreneurship, The University of Arizona
- » Marie Wesselhoft, President and Cofounder of MSDx
- » Steven Wood, Mentor, Arizona Center for Innovation

Production and Support

We would like to thank our partners for helping us create this workbook:
- » Dan Duncan, Gecko Broadcast Productions
- » Thomas Prentice, Workbook Project Coordinator

Workbook Publishing

1760 East River Road, Suite 145
Tucson, Arizona 85718
www.wheatmark.com

www.ingramcontent.com/pod-product-compliance
Lightning Source LLC
Chambersburg PA
CBHW081113170526
45165CB00008B/2440